Misjudging Separation Of Church And State

Other books authored by Michael T. Petro, Jr.

How to Protect Yourself, Home & Family from Violent Criminals (1996; Out-of-Print)

Welcome to Soviet America: Special Edition (2010)

How I Quit Smoking in 31 Days After Smoking for 32 Years! (2012)

Under Attack: How The Tea Party Can Fight Back & Win (2014) Coauthored with former Clinton advisor, Larry Nichols

Books edited by Michael T. Petro, Jr.

God Brings Life Out of Adversity, by Joann Berkhouse (2013)

Hey Gang! Ready to Go-Go? by Carey Masci (2014)

My Life, My Letters & My Loves: Exploring An Ordinary Life, by Alida Henriette Struze (2015)

What Is A Schizophrenic Supposed To Look Like? by Lori Rochat (2015)

What Is A Schizophrenic Supposed To Look Like? Second Edition, by Lori Rochat (2016)

Turkish Delights, by Joseph Patrick Meissner et al. (2016)

What Is A Schizophrenic Supposed To Look Like? Third Edition, by Lori Rochat (2017)

Misjudging Separation Of Church And State:

50 Bundled Facts

You Won't Learn At Harvard Law School Or Read In The New York Times!

Michael T. Petro, Jr.

Misjudging Separation Of Church And State:
50 Bundled Facts You Won't Learn At Harvard
Law School Or Read In The New York Times!

Author: Michael T. Petro, Jr.

Published by Petro Publications
Cleveland, Ohio USA
PetroPublications.com

Front Cover Photo: Thankful Pray
ID 52576976 © Viovita | Dreamstime.com

Back Cover Photo: Attractive Girl Pray
ID: 16259519 © Elwynn | Dreamstime.com

ISBN-10: 0-9650411-6-6

ISBN-13: 978-0-9650411-6-4

Dedication

This book is dedicated to the memory of my father and mother. It is further dedicated to all patriotic American citizens of this generation and all previous generations, who have risked their lives, limbs, livelihood, and liberty to challenge criminals at all levels, whether foreign or domestic, public or private. I salute those patriotic American culture warriors who are now rising to meet the current threat to truth and freedom within the United States of America!

Table Of Contents

Introduction

The U.S. Supreme Court has reversed itself partially or entirely more than 200 times in the past due to erroneous decisions. The list of reversed U.S. Supreme Court decisions is available for anyone to review at GPO.gov.[1] In this book the reader will find 50 undeniable facts (many of which have been censored) that demonstrate beyond all doubt that the U.S. Supreme Court is obviously wrong about the principle of "separation of church and state" and must once again reverse itself entirely. Upon reviewing the 50 facts contained in this book, it becomes clear that the U.S. Supreme Court is corrupt, and corrupt justices must be impeached and removed from the bench. The damage they have inflicted upon religious liberty in America since 1962 is incalculable!

For those who believe it is impossible to impeach corrupt, lawless judges, they need to visit the website of the Federal Judicial Center.[2] At that site the reader finds a list of 15 federal judges who have been impeached by Congress in the past. Of the 15 impeached federal judges, eight were convicted and removed from office; four were acquitted of the charges; and three resigned when faced with impeachment. So, 11 of the 15 impeached federal judges were removed from the bench. It has been done before! It should be done again!

The reader will also find that many of the facts provided in this book are not taught at Harvard Law School – nor at any other law school in America! In addition, it soon becomes clear to the reader that most of the facts are not available via *The New York Times* – nor any other newspaper in America! Lastly, the reader will sadly discover that most of the facts listed in this book are not even discussed by TV and radio talk show hosts – whether liberal or conservative!

Liberals do not discuss most of the facts presented in this book for obvious reasons: They don't want Americans to become aware that leftist judges have been deceitfully robbing them of their religious liberty since 1962. Moreover, they don't want Americans to know how and why their religious liberty is under constant assault by leftist judges, lawyers, law professors, and so-called journalists and civil rights activists. Truth could result in their political demise!

Conservatives do not discuss many of the facts presented in this book for very different reasons. Stated simply, most people in positions of power and influence on the political Right have been intimidated into silence! They will discuss in detail the less controversial facts listed in this book, but almost never discuss the more controversial ones. When discussing the more controversial facts presented in this book, they tend to "tiptoe around the edges," and never make them the centerpiece of any discussion. Moreover, nearly all people in positions of power and influence on the political Right are simply too fearful of reprisal and rejection to publicly discuss the formidable and pervasive sinister forces behind the Court's misjudgments regarding "separation of church and state."

For these reasons, the book you are now holding in your hands is truly unique – and invaluable!

Chapter One

Five U.S. Supreme Court Decisions
Regarding Separation of Church & State

In **1962** the U.S. Supreme Court ruled in the case of *Engle v. Vitale* that prayer in America's public schools was unconstitutional when directed by a state government.[1]

In **1963**, in *Abington v. Schempp*, the U.S. Supreme Court ruled that it was unconstitutional for the state to sponsor Bible reading or the praying of the Lord's Prayer in public schools.[2]

In **1980** the U.S. Supreme Court ruled in *Stone v. Graham* that it was unconstitutional for the Ten Commandments to be posted in a public school classroom.[3]

In **1992** the U.S. Supreme Court ruled in *Lee v. Weisman* that it was unconstitutional for the state to sponsor prayer at school promotional activities and graduation ceremonies.[4]

In **2000** the U.S. Supreme Court ruled in *Santa Fe Independent School District v. Doe* that student-led, student-initiated prayer before a football game was unconstitutional.[5]

Collectively, in the above five cases the U.S. Supreme Court ruled that prayer, Bibles, and the Ten Commandments must be banned from government schools based on a letter written by President Thomas Jefferson. In this letter Thomas Jefferson stated that the First Amendment to the U.S. Constitution established "a wall of separation between Church and State." Thus, according to the U.S. Supreme Court, in each of the above five cases the principle of "separation of church and state" had been violated, as discussed in detail below.

While the first U.S. Supreme Court ruling that prohibited the free exercise of religion occurred in 1962 in the case of *Engle v. Vitale*, the first U.S. Supreme Court case wherein "Jefferson's wall" was misjudged occurred in 1947 in the case of *Everson v. Board of Education*.[6] In this case the Court ruled that taxpayer reimbursement of public transportation for children attending private religious schools did not violate the U.S. Constitution, which was the primary issue presented to the Court.

However, the Court did conclude that the Establishment Clause of the First Amendment did erect "a wall of separation between church and state," but not as Thomas Jefferson had intended. It also ruled that, under the Due Process Clause of the Fourteenth Amendment, the Bill of Rights in the federal Constitution applied to the states as well as the federal government. Therefore, Thomas Jefferson's "wall," which was reportedly created by the Establishment Clause of the First Amendment, also applied to the states. However, "Jefferson's wall," as cited in 1947, did not explicitly prohibit the free exercise of religion on government property, whether federal or state!

In 1962 everything changed, and the U.S. Supreme Court was not only wrong in the five decisions rendered after 1947, but their decisions represented the exact opposite of the intent of the Framers of the First Amendment. As President Ronald Reagan[7] correctly stated, "The Constitution was never meant to prevent people from praying, its declared purpose was to protect their freedom to pray."

Below the reader will find an uncensored examination of 50 undeniable facts that demonstrate beyond all doubt that the U.S. Supreme Court had ruled erroneously in 1947, 1962, and beyond. The reader will also find rarely discussed evidence that exposes the destructive forces behind the judicial malpractice that wrongfully restricts freedom of religious expression on government property. Moreover, the 50 undeniable facts represent 50 valid reasons why Americans who wish to see a return to honest government at the federal level, must demand that U.S. Supreme Court justices honestly and accurately construe the U.S. Constitution and reverse blatantly erroneous rulings – or face impeachment and removal from the bench!

Chapter Two

The First 25 Undeniable Facts

Fact Number One:

Thomas Jefferson's 1802 Letter

**In Thomas Jefferson's 1802 letter his "separation
of church and state" protected the church
from the federal government, but it did not protect
the church from state governments, and it did
not protect any government from the church**

As stated above, in establishing the doctrine of "separation of
church and state" the U.S. Supreme Court made reference to a
letter written by Thomas Jefferson in 1802. In this letter, written
to the Danbury Baptist Association in Danbury, Connecticut,
Jefferson addressed concerns expressed by these religious
leaders regarding the infringement of their religious liberty by
their state legislature. These Baptist religious leaders stated,
"what religious privileges we enjoy (as a minor part of the State)
we enjoy as favors granted, and not as inalienable rights: and
these favors we receive at the expense of such degrading
acknowledgments, as are inconsistent with the rights of freemen."

The Baptists acknowledged the fact that Thomas Jefferson could
do very little to alleviate this state problem because "the
President of the United States is not the national legislator."

However, perhaps because Thomas Jefferson was the author of the *Virginia Statute for Religious Freedom*,[1] they hoped that his long history as a staunch defender of religious liberty would "shine and prevail through all these states and all the world."

In his letter Thomas Jefferson expressed sympathy regarding their concern for government established religions at the state level that may have a negative impact on various religions not endorsed by the state. However, he acknowledged that the "wall of separation between Church and State" established by the First Amendment to the U.S. Constitution prohibited the federal government from interfering in religious activities at the state level.

Some have also concluded that the Baptist leaders feared the First Amendment to the federal Constitution could be construed as granting freedom of religion, rather than acknowledging that it was a God-given, inalienable right which must be protected by the federal government. And if freedom of religion was truly government-given, then the federal government could regulate religion.

To alleviate these fears Thomas Jefferson wrote the following within the heart of his letter: "...I contemplate with sovereign reverence that act of the whole American people which declared that their legislature would 'make no law respecting an establishment of religion, or prohibiting the free exercise thereof,' thus building a wall of separation between Church and State."

As the President of the United States, Thomas Jefferson sought to alleviate the fears of the Danbury Baptist Association by stating that religion was free from federal regulation and federal interference because the First Amendment provided "a wall of separation between Church and State." Clearly, Jefferson was telling these religious leaders that the "wall" protected the church from the federal government; he did not say the "wall" protected the federal government – or any government – from the church. (See Appendix A to read the letter the Danbury Baptist Association sent to Thomas Jefferson; and see Appendix B to read Thomas Jefferson's entire response to the Danbury Baptist Association)

Fact Number Two:

No Danbury Letters of Protest

If members of the Danbury Baptist Association believed that "Jefferson's Wall" prevented them from praying, Bible reading, or posting the Ten Commandments on government property, there would have been letters of protest in America's archives

To interpret "Jefferson's wall" as prohibiting the free exercise of religion by banning prayer, Bibles, and the Ten Commandments on government property would have exacerbated the fears of the Danbury Baptist Association. But their fears were alleviated by "Jefferson's wall," as Jefferson had intended. There is no historical evidence to the contrary! American archives would be filled with letters condemning Jefferson had his letter implied

that his "wall of separation between Church and State" prohibited members of the Danbury Baptist Association from praying,
reading the Bible, or posting the Ten Commandments on
government property – or placed any other restrictions on the
religious liberties of the American people!

As anyone could easily discern, the First Amendment, as all other
Amendments in the Bill of Rights, places restrictions on the
federal government, not on the American people! This point is
discussed in detail under Fact Number Seventeen!

Because members of the Danbury Baptist Association did not
express concern about "Jefferson's wall," one may erroneously
conclude that they wrote a letter to the President of the United
States to express their fears or concerns that religious people
may pray on government property, may read the Bible on
government property, or may post the Ten Commandments on
government property!

But why would religious leaders fear that there may be too much
religious liberty in the United States of America when their goal,
as Christians, is to spread the Gospel of Jesus Christ around the
world? Are we to believe that these Christian religious leaders
wanted President Thomas Jefferson to limit the free exercise of
religion – and therefore were not surprised or disappointed when
his "wall" prohibited the free exercise of religion on government
property?

Fact Number Three:

Thomas Jefferson's Prayer

**While serving in his official capacity as
President of the United States of America,
Thomas Jefferson ended his letter with a short prayer**

The Danbury Baptists ended their letter to President Thomas Jefferson with a short prayer:

"And may the Lord preserve you safe from every evil and bring you at last to his Heavenly Kingdom through Jesus Christ our Glorious Mediator." (See Appendix A)

In response, while serving in his official capacity as President of the United States of America, Thomas Jefferson also ended his letter with a short prayer:

"I reciprocate your kind prayers for the protection and blessing of the common Father and Creator of man, and tender you for yourselves and your religious association, assurances of my high respect and esteem." (See Appendix B)

The U.S. Supreme Court is obviously wrong because by ending his letter with a prayer Thomas Jefferson would have contradicted his written words regarding the principle of "separation of church and state" as defined by the U.S. Supreme Court. This is just **one example** of the Court rendering Thomas Jefferson's behavior inexplicably contradictory!

Fact Number Four:

Thomas Jefferson's 1805
Second Inaugural Address

In Thomas Jefferson's 1805 *Second Inaugural Address* he reinforced the notion that the First Amendment protected the church from the state, not the state from the church

Those who misconstrue Jefferson's "wall of separation" should take note of his 1805 *Second Inaugural Address*[2] wherein he stated that, "In matters of religion I have considered that its free exercise is placed by the Constitution independent of the powers of the General [federal] Government. I have therefore undertaken on no occasion to prescribe the religious exercises suited to it, but have left them, as the Constitution found them, under the direction and discipline of the church or state authorities acknowledged by the several religious societies."

Later in this Address Jefferson added the following: "...that the public efforts may be directed honestly to the public good, that peace be cultivated, civil and religious liberty unassailed, law and order preserved..." So, "Jefferson's wall" left "religious liberty unassailed." Contrastingly, when the U.S. Supreme Court banned payer, the Bible, and the Ten Commandments on government property, it did not leave "religious liberty unassailed," as clearly advocated in Jefferson's 1805 *Second Inaugural Address*. This is the **second example** of the Court rendering Thomas Jefferson's behavior (his written and spoken words) inexplicably contradictory by their erroneous decisions regarding "separation of church and state."

John W. Whitehead[3] has noted that this 1805 Address by Thomas Jefferson clearly supports the notion that his "wall of separation between Church and State," as written earlier in 1802, was a wall erected around the church to protect it from any infringements by the federal government. Note that, as President, Thomas Jefferson stated the federal government had no authority over "religious exercises." Obviously, praying, Bible reading, and displaying the Ten Commandments are religious exercises over which the federal government has no authority. However, he further stated that individual state governments (many of which had established churches during Jefferson's lifetime) could exercise "direction and discipline" over religious expression as "acknowledged by the several religious societies."

Therefore, according to Thomas Jefferson, when people engage in praying, Bible reading, or the posting of the Ten Commandments as directed by state governments, the federal government has no constitutional authority to interfere with that practice! As noted above, in 1947 the U.S. Supreme Court applied the Fourteenth Amendment to the states, and thus cancelled out Thomas Jefferson's earlier position. In 1962 and beyond the U.S. Supreme Court concurred with the 1947 ruling, and not with Thomas Jefferson's earlier position. Their decisions are therefore not consistent with the words of Thomas Jefferson, but the complete opposite of his written words (and his actions, as described below!)

Thomas Jefferson's understanding of "separation of church and state" appears to be consistent with that of the other Founders, who may have feared the federal government may follow in the footsteps of the British Government and establish a national religion or national church, perhaps something akin to the Church of England. The Establishment Clause prevents this from occurring.

Fact Number Five:

James Madison on Church and State

James Madison also stated that the U.S. Constitution protects the church from the state

Thomas Jefferson's *Second Inaugural Address* is consistent with statements of James Madison,[4] the fourth President of the United States, the "Father of the U.S. Constitution," and the primary author of the First Amendment who said, "There is not a shadow of right in the General [federal] Government to intermeddle with religion...This subject is, for the honor of America, perfectly free and unshackled. The government has no jurisdiction over it." In other words, the federal government has no authority to prohibit the free exercise of religion on federal government property – or any property!

Fact Number Six:

James Madison on Religious Liberty

James Madison also stated that
"separation of church and state"
increased, rather than decreased,
religious liberty

James Madison[5] wrote the following to Robert Welsh, Jr. in 1819: "Whilst the number, the industry, and the morality of the priest-hood and the devotion of the people have been manifestly increased by the total separation of the Church from the State." So, Madison said that separation of church and state increased religious liberty, but the U.S. Supreme Court has stated that "separation of church and state" must decrease religious liberty. Who should we believe, the primary author of the Establishment Clause of the First Amendment or the U.S. Supreme Court?

Fact Number Seven:

Thomas Jefferson and
the University of Virginia

Thomas Jefferson encouraged prayer
by students and professors at the
public University of Virginia

It must also be noted that, in his superb 1982 book, *The Second American Revolution*, John W. Whitehead[6] reported that Thomas Jefferson not only founded the University of Virginia, but he also encouraged students to meet, pray, and worship together on campus. Jefferson further encouraged students to meet and pray on campus with their professors. Keep in mind the University of Virginia is a public educational institution, and according to the

14

U.S. Supreme Court, praying, Bible reading, and the posting of the Ten Commandments are forbidden on such property – based on one letter written by Thomas Jefferson.

Once again, the U.S. Supreme Court is obviously wrong because this behavior by Thomas Jefferson would have contradicted his written words regarding the principle of "separation of church and state." This is the **third example** of seemingly contradictory behavior by Thomas Jefferson created by the U.S. Supreme Court's erroneous decisions.

How can the U.S. Supreme Court rule that Thomas Jefferson's "wall" forbids students and teachers from praying on government property when Thomas Jefferson encouraged students and professors to pray together on government property?

Fact Number Eight:

Thomas Jefferson and the Washington Public Schools

Thomas Jefferson encouraged the use of the Bible and the Isaac Watts Hymnal as teaching aids in Washington Public Schools

John W. Whitehead[7] also noted that Thomas Jefferson authored the first plan of public education, which was adopted by the city of Washington. In this public educational plan for the city of Washington, President Thomas Jefferson recommended the employment of the Bible and the Isaac Watts Hymnal as teaching aides to help students learn how to read.

The U.S. Supreme Court is clearly wrong because this behavior by Thomas Jefferson would have contradicted his written words regarding the principle of "separation of church and state." This is a **fourth example** of such a contradiction.

How can the U.S. Supreme Court rule that Thomas Jefferson's "wall" forbids the use of the Bible on government property when Thomas Jefferson encouraged the use of the Bible on government property?

Fact Number Nine:

Thomas Jefferson and
Sunday Church Services

**Thomas Jefferson routinely attended Sunday
church services on federal government property**

Many of the Framers of the U.S. Constitution engaged in prayer on government property. As stated elsewhere in this book, it is a practice that continues to this day in the U.S. Senate and U.S. House of Representatives. In addition, it should also be noted that Thomas Jefferson attended non-denominational Christian church services on Sundays inside the U.S. Capitol – which, for decades, was converted into a church on Sundays precisely for Christian worship services! Thus, one day each week for several decades church and state were merged together as one, indivisible entity – and this was approved by Thomas Jefferson.[8, 9, 10] So, for many years Thomas Jefferson prayed on federal government property every Sunday, but the U.S. Supreme Court has repeatedly told us that Thomas Jefferson believed it was unconstitutional for prayer to occur on federal government property! What a monumental travesty of justice!

Once again, the U.S. Supreme Court is obviously incorrect because this behavior by Thomas Jefferson would have contra-dicted his written words regarding the principle of "separation of church and state." This is a **fifth example** of such a contradict-tion.

How can the U.S. Supreme Court rule that Thomas Jefferson believed it was unconstitutional for students and teachers to pray on government property when Thomas Jefferson prayed on government property for several decades?

Fact Number Ten:

James Madison and
Sunday Church Services

James Madison routinely attended Sunday church services on federal government property

James Madison,[11] the "Father of the U.S. Constitution," and the primary author of the First Amendment, attended non-denominational Christian church services on Sundays inside the U.S. Capitol along with Thomas Jefferson. Yet, we are told that James Madison, along with Thomas Jefferson, believed religious activities on government property was unconstitutional.

How can the U.S. Supreme Court rule that the Establishment Clause forbids students and teachers from praying on government property when the primary author of the Establishment Clause prayed on government property?

Fact Number Eleven:

Our Founding Fathers and the Bible

**Our Founding Fathers
used the Bible on government property
to conduct official government business,
along with various forms of prayer**

A 1767 King James Bible was used during the oath of office ceremony of George Washington, the first President of the United States of America, and "The Father of our country." For the ceremony, the Bible was brought by Jacob Morton onto government property, notably the old City Hall in New York City, which was later called Federal Hall.[12]

The U.S. Constitution, Article II, Section 1, states the following regarding the oath of office for the incoming President of the United States:

"Before he enter on the execution of his office, he shall take the following oath or affirmation: 'I do solemnly swear (or affirm) that I will faithfully execute the office of the President of the United States, and will to the best of my ability, preserve, protect, and defend the Constitution of the United States.'"

George Washington, the first to take the presidential oath of office, placed his left hand on the opened Bible as he spoke. He ended his sworn statement with "So help me God." He also bent over and kissed the Bible[13] So, who was George Washington addressing when he said "So help me God?" Clearly, he was addressing God. One may conclude that he was either asking God for help, which is a form of prayer, or affirming to God that he will faithfully execute his duties as our first President, which is also a form of prayer! In either case George Washington was talking to God – which is the very definition of prayer! Is this not a violation of the principle of "separation of church and state" as later established by the U.S. Supreme Court?

"So Help me God" – What does it mean?

An examination of the phrase "So help me God" can be reviewed at americancreation.blogspot.com.[14] Citing the *William and Mary Law Review (1992)*, "So help me God" is an abbreviated form of the following oath: "So may God help me at the judgment day if I speak true, but if I speak false, then may He withdraw His help from me." Ray Soller, the author at *American Creation*, further noted that oaths have roots in the Bible, and several examples are provided at the above website.

In addition Ray Soller cites James Endell Tyler who authored *Oaths: their origin, nature, and history (1834)* wherein he found the following definition of an oath: "An oath is an outward pledge given by the juror that his attestation [or promise] is made under an immediate sense of his responsibility to God." This definition includes "an immediate sense of responsibility to

God" because oaths taken by jurors at the federal level and at the state level usually end with the words, "So help me God."

Thereafter subsequent Founding Fathers took the oath of office as President with a Bible on government property. This included John Adams, the second President of the United States who championed the inclusion of the Bill of Rights in the U.S. Constitution, and Thomas Jefferson, the third President of the United States who authored the words "wall of separation between church and state." Once again it must be said, the U.S. Supreme Court is clearly mistaken because this behavior by Thomas Jefferson would have contradicted his written words regarding the principle of "separation of church and state." This is the **sixth example** of such a contradiction.

The Bible was also used on government property for the oath of office ceremony of James Madison, the fourth President of the United States, the "Father of the U.S. Constitution" and primary author of the First Amendment and the words, "Congress shall make no law respecting an establishment of religion, or prohibiting the free exercise thereof; or abridging the freedom of speech or of the press; or the right of the people peaceably to assemble, and to petition the Government for a redress of grievances."

Clearly, our Founding Fathers had no problem employing the Bible (which contains the Ten Commandments) on government property to conduct official government business – such as oath-taking by the President of the United States – a practice that has been honored by nearly all U.S. presidents – and continues to this day! Most importantly, both early American presidents and current presidents have had no problem publicly invoking God to hold them responsible for the manner in which they subsequently honor their oaths of office!

How can the U.S. Supreme Court rule that the Establishment Clause forbids students and teachers from praying on government property when many of our Founding Fathers prayed on government property?

Fact Number Twelve:

America's Founding Documents

**"Separation of church and state"
cannot be found in any of
America's founding documents**

The words "separation of church and state" cannot be found anywhere in the U.S. Constitution, nor in the Declaration of Independence, nor in any other founding American documents. Nor can we find any wording that remotely resembles "separation of church and state" in our founding documents.

As noted at Wallbuilders,[15] the construction of the First Amendment occurred from June 7, 1789 to September 25, 1789. The debates among the 90 Founding Fathers who framed the First Amendment were recorded in the *Congressional Records* during that four month period. However, over this extended period of time none of the 90 Framers of the First Amendment ever used the words "separation of church and state."

Fact Number Thirteen:

The Framers of the First Amendment

**Thomas Jefferson was not
one of the Framers of
the First Amendment**

In addition to the above, although Thomas Jefferson[16] did employ the words "separation between church and state" some 12 years after the 1789 First Amendment debates occurred, he was not one of the 90 Framers of the First Amendment to the U.S. Constitution who engaged in those debates!

So why do members of the U.S. Supreme Court choose to use the words of Thomas Jefferson over the words of the actual Framers of the First Amendment? This fact alone calls into question the judgment (and integrity) of the U.S. Supreme Court!

Fact Number Fourteen:

The Northwest Ordinance of 1787

**The Congressmen who embraced the
First Amendment and the Establishment Clause
stated in the Northwest Ordinance of 1787
that religion was necessary for good government**

In 1787 the Congress of the Confederation of the United States passed the Northwest Ordinance. This act by Congress created the Northwest Territory of the United States, which would later become the states of Ohio, Indiana, Illinois, Michigan, Wisconsin, and part of Minnesota. When the Articles of Confederation were replaced with the U.S. Constitution in 1789, the Northwest Ordinance was modified slightly and replaced with the Northwest Ordinance of 1789.

Article 3 of the Northwest Ordinance of 1787 states the following: "Religion, morality, and knowledge, being necessary to good government and the happiness of mankind, schools and the means of education shall forever be encouraged." Keep in mind the Congress which created the Northwest Ordinance of 1787 was composed of essentially the same people who composed the Congress of 1791. Most importantly, it was this Congress of 1791 which added the Bill of Rights, and thus the First Amendment and the Establishment Clause, to the U.S. Constitution[17, 18, 19]

So, the congressmen who said "Religion, morality, and knowledge, being necessary to good government..." are the same congressmen who added the First Amendment and the Establishment Clause to the U.S. Constitution. Based on this one piece of evident alone, any honest person must conclude that the Establishment Clause was not adopted to keep religion out of government, given the fact that the men who embraced the Establishment Clause stated earlier that religion was necessary for good government! Stated as simply as possible, why would congressmen keep religion out of government when they clearly proclaimed that religion was necessary for good government?

How can the U.S. Supreme Court rule that the Establishment Clause forbids religion on government property when the

congressmen responsible for the adoption of the Establishment
Clause stated that religion was necessary for good government?

Fact Number Fifteen:

Our Founding Fathers
and Biblical Foundation

Many Founding Fathers believed
government would become corrupt
without a biblical foundation

Ignoring the wording of the First Amendment, the original intent,
and the recorded words and actions of the Framers of the U.S.
Constitution, the U.S. Supreme Court came to the preposterous
conclusion that the Christians who drafted the First Amendment
intended to establish a "wall of separation" to keep religion out
of government. What kind of mind would conclude that
America's Christian Founders, who believed government could
not succeed without biblical principles, would keep biblical principles out of the government they just created?

Read just a few quotes from some of our Founding Fathers and
ask yourself, did they believe that prayer, the Bible, and the Ten
Commandments had no place in government?

One: "Our Constitution was made only for a moral and religious
people. It is wholly inadequate for the government of any other."
– **John Adams**.[20] Second President of the United States of
America, signer of the Declaration of Independence, and signer
of the Bill of Rights.

Two: "Providence has given to our people the choice of their rulers, and it is the duty as well as the privilege and interest of our Christian nation, to select and prefer Christians for their rulers..." – **John Jay**[21] President of the Continental Congress and first Chief Justice of the U.S. Supreme Court.

Three: "The great pillars of all government and of social life [are] virtue, morality, and religion. This is the armor, my friend, and this alone, that renders us invincible." – **Patrick Henry**,[22] Continental Army officer; helped pave the way for the Bill of Rights in the U.S. Constitution; immortalized the phrase "Give me liberty, or give me death!"

Four: "[T]he only means of establishing and perpetuating our republican forms of government is the universal education of our youth in the principles of Christianity by means of the Bible." And, "The Bible, when not read in schools, is seldom read in any subsequent period of life... [T]he Bible... should be read in our schools in preference to all other books because it contains the greatest portion of that kind of knowledge which is calculated to produce private and public happiness." – **Benjamin Rush**,[23] Signatory to the Declaration of Independence; helped ratify the U.S. Constitution; and, "Father of public schools under the Constitution."

Five: "[T]he Christian religion is the most important and one of the first things in which all children under a free government ought to be instructed. No truth is more evident than that the Christian religion must be the basis of any government intended to secure the rights and privileges of a free people." – **Noah**

Webster,[24] Member of the Connecticut Militia during the American Revolution; later authored early American dictionaries

Six: "Whenever the pillars of Christianity shall be overthrown, our present republican forms of government – and all the blessings which flow from them – must fall with them." – **Jedidiah Morse**,[25] a youth during the American Revolution; became an Historian of the American Revolution

How can the U.S. Supreme Court rule that the Establishment Clause forbids the use of the Bible on government property when our Founding Fathers stated that government would become corrupt if not based on biblical principles?

Fact Number Sixteen:

Misjudging the Authors of the First Amendment

In rendering these five decisions, the U.S. Supreme Court concluded that the authors of the First Amendment did not understand the meaning of the words contained within the First Amendment regarding freedom of religion

The U.S. Constitution was drafted in 1787, and the Bill of Rights, which is the first Ten Amendments, was ratified in 1791. But in each of the above five decisions the U.S. Supreme Court put forth the preposterous conclusion that, from 1791 to 1962, everyone, including those who authored the First Amendment, did not understand the meaning of the words in the First Amendment.

We are to believe that for 171 years the First Amendment had been misunderstood, and George Washington, James Madison, Alexander Hamilton, Benjamin Franklin, and the other 35 signatories to the U.S. Constitution misunderstood the document they created because they frequently prayed on government property (and some attended church services on government property, as explored above in Facts Number Nine and Ten). Are we to believe that the Court finally corrected their mistaken understanding of the document our Founding Fathers created? Such a conclusion is patently absurd!

Fact Number Seventeen:

No Restrictions on "We the People"

**The First Amendment to the U.S. Constitution,
as all other Amendments in the Bill of Rights,
places restrictions on the U.S. Government,
and places no restrictions on "We the People"**

As discussed earlier, the Establishment Clause of the **First Amendment** to the U.S. Constitution clearly states that, "Congress shall make no law respecting an establishment of religion." It further states that Congress shall make no law "prohibiting the free exercise thereof; or abridging the freedom of speech or of the press; or the right of the people peaceably to assemble, and to petition the Government for a redress of grievances."

What is clearly stated is that the federal government may not establish a religion, and it may not prohibit Americans from freely engaging in religious activities – such as praying, Bible reading, or posting of the Ten Commandments. A careful reading of the entire Bill of Rights reveals that it places restrictions on the U.S. Government, but places no restrictions on "We the People."

The First Amendment makes no mention of the President nor the U.S. Supreme Court because neither has the constitutional authority to make law. The U.S. Constitution gives all lawmaking power to Congress, which is the legislative branch of the federal government. The President, as the head of the executive branch, is to faithfully execute the laws created by Congress, and the U.S. Supreme Court, which is the judicial branch, is to resolve disputes as outlined in Article III of the U.S. Constitution.

According to Mark R. Levin and others, the U.S. Supreme Court granted to itself the power to render decisions regarding the constitutionality of legislation passed by Congress and signed by the President. Such power, referred to as "Judicial Review," was not delegated to the Court in the U.S. Constitution, but was simply adopted by the Court in the 1803 case of *Marbury v. Madison*.[26] (See Appendix C to read the entire text of Article III of the U.S. Constitution which outlines the powers delegated to the U.S. Supreme Court)

Let's look at the obvious restrictions placed on Congress, and thus the federal government, regarding other Amendments in the Bill of Rights: (See Appendix D for a complete list of the Bill of Rights)

The **Second Amendment** says, "A well regulated militia, being necessary to the security of a free State, the right of the people to keep and bear Arms, shall not be infringed." Shall not be infringed by whom? By the federal government! The federal government shall not infringe, nor restrict, limit, or undermine, the right of the people to keep and bear arms.

The **Third Amendment** says the federal government shall not quarter soldiers in the homes of citizens in peacetime without the consent of the owner, nor during wartime – except as prescribed by law. This is an obvious restriction on the federal government.

The **Fourth Amendment** says the right of the people to be secure in their persons, houses, papers, and effects, against unreasonable searches and seizures, shall not be violated by the federal government. Clearly, this is another restriction on the federal government, not the American people.

The **Fifth Amendment** restricts the government in many ways. For example, we have all watched TV courtroom scenes wherein a defendant pleads the "Fifth Amendment." By doing so he publicly states that, as guaranteed by the Fifth Amendment, the government may not force the individual to testify against himself – thus he cannot be forced to be a witness against himself. Recently we saw Lois Lerner plead the Fifth Amendment when called before Congress to explain the IRS harassment of conservative organizations that applied for non-profit, tax-exempt status during the Obama Administration! The federal government was prohibited from forcing her to be a witness against herself.

The **Sixth Amendment** was designed to restrict the ability of government to convene "Show Trials" or "Kangaroo Courts," which would decrease the chances of a fair trial. It requires, for example, a speedy, public trial, an impartial jury, the right to legal counsel, the right to be confronted by accusers, etc., all of which cannot be restricted by government.

You get the idea! Each Amendment restricts the power of the federal government to prevent it from interfering with the natural, inalienable rights of the American people! As Thomas Jefferson has stated, the U.S. Constitution binds the federal government, and thus frees the American people:

"...in questions of power then, let no more be heard of confidence in man, but bind him down from mischief by the chains of the Constitution..." – Thomas Jefferson[27]

Barack Obama Acknowledged the U.S. Constitution Restricts Government, Not the People

As a matter of fact, as an Illinois state senator, Barack Obama acknowledged that the U.S. Constitution places restrictions on the federal government – and not on "We the People." Below is a transcript of Barack Obama's statements[28] regarding the limitations of government authority during a radio interview on January 18, 2001:

"But, the Supreme Court never ventured into the issues of redistribution of wealth and sort of more basic issues of political and economic justice in this society. And to that extent, as radical as I think people tried to characterize the Warren Court, it wasn't that radical. It didn't break free from the essential constraints that were placed by the Founding Fathers in the Constitution, at least as it's been interpreted, and [sic] Warren Court interpreted in the same way that, generally, the Constitution is a charter of negative liberties, says what the states can't do to you, says what the federal government can't do to you, but it doesn't say what the federal government or the state government must do on your behalf..."

The last sentence in Barack Obama's above statement is clearly incorrect. The U.S. Constitution does state what the federal government must do on our behalf. In Article I, Section 8 of the U.S. Constitution we find a list of 18 duties (or enumerated powers) the U.S. Congress is to perform on behalf of the states and the people, such as raising and supporting U.S. military forces, establishing Post Offices, regulating commerce, coining money, etc. (The federal duty of coining money was delegated to the Federal Reserve System, which is consistent with the central bank called for by Karl Marx in *The Communist Manifesto*!)

Moreover, the **Tenth Amendment** limits the federal government to those 18 duties. That's why the U.S. Supreme Court never "ventured into the issues of redistribution of wealth" or "political and economic justice" – as Barack Obama opined. Under the Tenth Amendment, the Court has no constitutional authority to do so. The Tenth Amendment reads as follows:

"The powers not delegated to the United States by the Constitution, nor prohibited by it to the States, are reserved to the States respectively or to the people."

In his statement Obama admitted that the U.S. Constitution outlines what the federal government "can't do to you," such as redistributing your money for "political and economic justice." And, he expressed remorse that the U.S. Supreme Court did not violate the U.S. Constitution to achieve those ends! And we are told that Obama lectured classes on constitutional law at the University of Chicago Law School from 1992 to 1996. How sad!

In acknowledging what the federal government "can't do to you" because of the restrictions placed upon it by the U.S. Constitution, Obama was inadvertently acknowledging that the federal government cannot prohibit the free exercise of religion, cannot prohibit the right of free speech, and cannot prohibit the right of the people to keep and bear arms, etc.

Fact Number Eighteen:

The Free Exercise Clause

The five decisions of the U.S. Supreme Court regarding "separation of church and state" place the Establishment Clause in direct conflict with the Free Exercise Clause of the First Amendment

The Free Exercise Clause states that Congress, and thus the federal government, shall not prohibit the free exercise of religion – anywhere at any time. No exceptions are listed. But by prohibiting prayer, Bible reading, and the posting of the Ten Commandments, the federal government forcibly prohibits the free exercise of religion. This is an obvious violation of the Free

Exercise Clause which states "Congress shall make no law... prohibiting the free exercise thereof." (Meaning Congress shall make no law prohibiting the free exercise of religion) The five Court rulings discussed above clearly render the First Amendment internally inconsistent, making the Establishment Clause contradict the Free Exercise Clause.

Fact Number Nineteen:

The Freedom of Speech Clause

The five decisions of the U.S. Supreme Court regarding "separation of church and state" place the Establishment Clause in direct conflict with the Freedom of Speech Clause of the First Amendment

The First Amendment also states that Congress, and thus the federal government, shall make no law "abridging the freedom of speech or of the press." From an American perspective, voluntary, spoken prayer, as traditionally said at school graduations, football games, and in public school classrooms, would most certainly be deemed the type of "free speech" which the federal government may not abridge. Prohibiting voluntary prayer or voluntary Bible reading clearly abridges freedom of speech. Once again, the five U.S. Supreme Court rulings render the First Amendment internally inconsistent by making the Establishment Clause contradict the Freedom of Speech Clause.

Fact Number Twenty:

Inside the U.S. Capitol Building

**There is a prayer room
inside the U.S. Capitol Building**

Did you know that near the Rotunda of the U.S. Capitol there is an official prayer room? It is not open to the public, and is used by U.S. Senators and Representatives as a quiet place for individual meditation and prayer. In 1954 the prayer room was established with passage of House Concurrent Resolution 60. It was supported by both the House and the Senate, and the prayer room opened for use in 1955 – seven years before the U.S. Supreme Court began prohibiting the free exercise of religion on government property in violation of the Free Exercise Clause and the Free Speech Clause of the First Amendment.

The Congressional Prayer Room[29] contains a stained glass window with the image of George Washington kneeling in prayer. Around him we find the following printed words: "Preserve me, O God, for in thee do I put my trust." (Psalm 16:1) Above George Washington are the following words of Abraham Lincoln: "This Nation Under God."

Under the window in the Congressional Prayer Room one finds an alter, and upon the alter sits the Bible, usually opened to Psalm 23, which reads as follows:

"The Lord is my shepherd; I shall not want. He maketh me to lie down in green pastures: he leadeth me beside the still waters. He

11

restoreth my soul: he leadeth me in the paths of righteousness for his name's sake, Yea, though I walk through the valley of the shadow of death, I will fear no evil: for thou art with me; they rod and thy staff they comfort me. Thou prepares a table before me in the presence of mine enemies: thou anointest my head with oil; my cup runneth over. Surely goodness and mercy shall follow me all the days of my life: and I will dwell in the house of the Lord for ever."

Fact Number Twenty-One:

A Soviet Constitutional Principle

**"Separation of church and state"
is a Soviet constitutional principle**

While the words "separation of church and state" cannot be found in any of America's founding documents, Article 52 of the 1977 Soviet Constitution stated the following: "Citizens of the USSR are guaranteed freedom of conscience, that is, the right to profess or not to profess any religion, and to conduct religious worship or atheistic propaganda. Incitement of hostility or hatred on religious grounds is prohibited. In the USSR, the church is separated from the state, and the school from the church." Similar Articles were placed in the 1936 Soviet Constitution and the 1993 Russian Federation Constitution. Based upon their rulings, one may conclude that the U.S. Supreme Court has been employing the Soviet constitutional principle of "separation of church and state" and fraudulently transplanting it into the U.S. Constitution. (See Appendix E, Separation of Church And State In The Soviet And Russian Constitutions)

Fact Number Twenty-Two:

"We the People" are the Masters

The Declaration of Independence and the U.S. Constitution establish "We the People" as the masters and government officials as our servants

"The saddest epitaph which can be carved in memory of a vanished liberty is that it was lost because its possessors failed to stretch forth a saving hand while yet there was time." – George Sutherland, Supreme Court Justice[30]

By imposing the Soviet constitutional principle of "separation of church and state" upon us through Court decisions, the "justices" have reversed the relationship of government to "We the People." Our Declaration of Independence and Constitution establish the principle that politicians and judges are the servants and "We the People" are the masters. (Keep in mind the states created the federal government to be a servant to the states and to the people. The states did not create the federal government to usurp their legitimate power, rule over them, and micro-manage their internal affairs)

Abraham Lincoln, our 16th President, acknowledged this relation-ship when he said in America we have, "government of the people, by the people, and for the people."[31] President Lincoln was even more explicit when he stated that, "The people of these United States are the rightful masters of both Congresses and courts, not to overthrow the Constitution, but to overthrow the men who pervert that Constitution."[32]

Ronald Reagan,[33] our 40th President, concurred when he said, "The Founding Fathers understood that only by making government the servant, and not the master, only by positing sovereignty in the people and not in the state can we hope to protect freedom and see the political commonwealth prosper."

The President, Congress, and the courts, have been established as servants to "We the People." So how can our government servants tell us, their masters, where we can and cannot pray, read the Bible, post the Ten Commandments, erect crosses and other Christian symbols, or engage in any other religious activity on public property that is financed by our tax dollars?

Fact Number Twenty-Three:

Irrational Restrictions on "We the People"

The five decisions of the U.S. Supreme Court regarding "separation of church and state" lead to irrational restrictions on "We the People"

When reviewing the above Court decisions regarding the Establishment Clause of the First Amendment to the U.S. Constitution, consider the following: Forbidding students, or anyone else, from voluntarily praying, reading the Bible, or posting the Ten Commandments on government property simply does not pass any test of common sense – from an American perspective! Stated simply, it means a taxpayer cannot pray on taxpayer-funded property!

This could only make sense to those who view religious liberty from the perspective of Karl Marx, Vladimir Lenin, Joseph Stalin, and Nikita Khrushchev, but not from the perspective of George Washington, John Adams, Thomas Jefferson, and James Madison. This could only make sense to those who are guided by principles that are found in the Soviet Constitution – and could never make sense to individuals inspired by the principles found in the U.S. Constitution!

Fact Number Twenty-Four:

Students and Teachers Equated
with Members of Congress

The five decisions of the U.S. Supreme Court regarding "separation of church and state" falsely equate students and teachers with members of Congress

To say that a student praying on government property violates the Establishment Clause is to say that the student is a member of Congress attempting to establish a national religion or a national church. But the praying student is not a government official of any kind, and may not even be a member of any religion or a member of any church. This same principle holds true for teachers and other school officials. To assert that a private, taxpaying citizen engaging in voluntary prayer on taxpayer-funded property somehow violates a constitutional restriction that was placed on the federal government is clearly symptomatic of dishonest or irrational thought processes. As stated in the U.S. Constitution for anyone to read, the student or teacher is someone who possesses a right to religious expression that cannot be prohibited by Congress, and therefore cannot be prohibited by the President, the U.S. Supreme Court, or any other federal officials.

Bishop E. W. Jackson, Sr.[34] of the Exodus Faith Ministries in Chesapeake, Virginia points out the obvious lack of logic behind the notion that, for example, Bible reading or praying before a football game could possibly violate the First Amendment:

"What does the First Amendment say? The First Amendment says, 'Congress shall make no law.'"

"So, to me, if a local school engages in Bible study, Bible reading, or prayer, it is because of the culture of that local community says, 'that's what we want.' And culture is not Congress. Does that make sense? The First Amendment says '*Congress* shall make no law.'"

So, while the author of this book noted that the defenders of the Soviet constitutional principle of "separation of church and state" falsely equate students and teachers with members of Congress, Bishop Jackson points out that they (he was referring to the ACLU) falsely equate American culture with Congress. Both conclusions correctly point out the irrationality of such Court decisions.

Bishop Jackson further stated that, "How is it a law if a local sports team says, 'okay, we're going to pray before the game?' A public school sports team says 'we're going to pray before the game because it's a dangerous game, we're playing football, we don't want anyone to be injured, we want God to take care of us all, let's pray.'"

I would like the reader to ponder the following two questions: What federal law is established by Congress when students and teachers voluntarily pray at a public school before a football game? What federal law is established by Congress when private citizen taxpayers voluntarily pray on taxpayer-funded property?

Fact Number Twenty-Five:

Prayer in the U.S. Senate

Members of the U.S. Senate pray together on government property before each session begins

As stated earlier, in 1962 the U.S. Supreme Court ruled in the case of *Engle v. Vitale* that prayer in America's public schools was unconstitutional when directed by a state government. In 1963, in *Abington v. Schempp*, the U.S. Supreme Court ruled that it was unconstitutional for the state to sponsor Bible reading or the praying of the Lord's Prayer in public schools. Consequently, the ACLU and other organizations that support the Soviet constitutional principle of "separation of church and state" have been scouring the country and suing and threatening to sue taxpayers who pray on taxpayer-funded property!

These two Court decisions were rendered in contradiction to the fact that the U.S. Senate opens each session with prayer.

According to Mildred Amer,[35] "The custom of opening legislative sessions with a prayer began in the Continental Congress, which elected Jacob Duche, Rector of Christ Episcopal Church in Phila-delphia, to serve as its chaplain from 1774 to 1776. Except for a brief period..., both chambers have elected a chaplain since the First Congress in 1789."

Why is it constitutional for U.S. Senators to pray on government property, but unconstitutional for students and teachers to pray on government property? Why does the U.S. Supreme Court discriminate against students and teachers in this manner?

Chapter Three

The Second 25 Undeniable Facts

Fact Number Twenty-Six:

Chaplains in the U.S. Senate

The U.S. Senate has its own taxpayer-funded chaplin to lead its members in prayer on government property before each session begins

The opening prayer held in the U.S. Senate before each session begins is led by the Senate chaplain.[1] U.S. Senate chaplain candidates are chosen by the leadership of the U.S. Senate, and ultimately selected through an election process. As of 2008 there have been 62 Senate chaplains, and as of that date, the Senate chaplain receives an annual salary of $146,600 – paid for with U.S. taxpayer dollars![2]

Why is it constitutional for U.S. Senate chaplains to pray on government property, but unconstitutional for students and teachers to pray on government property? Why does the U.S. Supreme Court discriminate against students and teachers in this manner?

Fact Number Twenty-Seven:

Prayer in the U.S. House of Representatives

Members of the U.S. House of Representatives
pray together on government property
before each session begins

Consistent with the U.S. Senate, the U.S. House of Representatives also opens each session with prayer[3] Again, this federal
tradition dates back to 1774 when the Continental Congress was
held in Philadelphia, Pennsylvania, and each session was opened
with prayer.

Why is it constitutional for U.S. Representatives to pray on
government property, but unconstitutional for students and
teachers to pray on government property? Why does the U.S.
Supreme Court discriminate against students and teachers in this
manner?

Fact Number Twenty-Eight:

Chaplains in the U.S. House of Representatives

The U.S. House of Representatives has its own
taxpayer-funded chaplain to lead its members
in prayer on government property
before each session begins

The opening prayer held in the U.S. House of Representatives
before each session begins is led by the House chaplain.[4] The

43

House chaplain candidates are chosen by the leadership of the House, and ultimately selected through an election process. Unlike the Senate chaplain, the House chaplain is elected for a two-year term at the beginning of each new Congress. As of 2008 there have been 59 House chaplains, and as of that date, the House chaplain receives an annual salary of $167,800 – paid for with U.S. taxpayer dollars![5]

Why is it constitutional for U.S. House chaplains to pray on government property, but unconstitutional for students and teachers to pray on government property? Why does the U.S. Supreme Court discriminate against students and teachers in this manner?

Fact Number Twenty-Nine:

Prayer in State Legislatures

**Almost all state legislatures
pray on government property
before each session begins**

According to the National Conference of State Legislatures, "Almost all state legislatures still use an opening prayer as part of their tradition and procedure." Some have established guidelines to be followed, which may indicate who can lead the group in prayer and when the prayer is to be delivered.[6]

Why is it constitutional state legislators to pray on government property, but unconstitutional for students and teachers to pray on government property? Why does the U.S. Supreme Court discriminate against students and teachers in this manner?

Fact Number Thirty:

Chaplains in State Legislatures

Many state legislatures have their own taxpayer-funded chaplains to lead them in prayer on government property before each session begins

Consistent with the U.S. Senate and U.S. House of Representatives, most state Senate and House legislative bodies have chaplains. And, like the federal legislatures, many state legislatures fund their chaplains with taxpayer money. A few do not compensate their chaplains. Some state legislatures use visiting chaplains, and some states legislatures provide compensation to visiting chaplains while others do not.[7]

Why is it constitutional for state chaplains to pray on government property, but unconstitutional for students and teachers to pray on government property? Why does the U.S. Supreme Court discriminate against students and teachers in this manner?

Fact Number Thirty-One:

Marsh v. Chambers (1983)

**The Phenomenon of *Marsh v. Chambers*
demonstrates that the U.S. Supreme Court
is arbitrary and inconsistent in its rulings
regarding "separation of church and state"**

In 1983 both opponents of, and supporters of, the Soviet constitutional principle of "separation of church and state" were mystified by the ruling of the U.S. Supreme Court in the case of *Marsh v. Chambers.* By a vote of 6 to 3, the U.S. Supreme Court ruled it was not unconstitutional for state legislatures to open each session with prayer. The Court ruled that such prayer did not violate the Establishment Clause in the First Amendment to the U.S. Constitution – even when state funds were used to employ a Christian chaplain to lead state legislators in prayer!

Interestingly, the Court concluded that government funding for chaplains was constitutional because of the "unique history" of the United States of America. In 1791, just three days before the ratification of the Bill of Rights – and thus the First Amendment, the federal legislature authorized the employment of a chaplain to lead the legislators in prayer. Therefore, the Court concluded, those who ratified the Bill of Rights saw no violation of the Establishment Clause when each session was opened with prayer which was led by a paid chaplin.[8, 9, 10]

As we have often heard, even a stopped clock is correct twice each day! Therefore, even a corrupt Court can occasionally render a logical decision that is consistent with the U.S. Constitution! However, the same logic used in *Marsh v. Chambers* should be applied by the Court in all cases regarding the Establishment Clause and the principle of "separation of church and state!"

Fact Number Thirty-Two:

The CPUSA and Religion

The National Chairman of the Communist Party, USA predicted in 1932 that a Soviet-style government would prohibit the free exercise of religion in America's public schools

In 1932 William Z. Foster, the National Chairman of the Communist Party, USA, (CPUSA) wrote a book titled *Toward Soviet America*. In his book Foster revealed the Communist plan to build a Soviet America, or an American version of the Soviet Union. (This topic is examined in detail in the book, *Welcome to Soviet America: Special Edition*) Foster provided the reader with a general plan with many specific details. Among the many details provided by Foster we find the following: In Soviet America "God will be banished from the laboratories as well as from the schools."[11] Communist William Z. Foster further predicted that, in Soviet American schools, "The studies will be revolutionized, being cleansed of religious, patriotic and other features of the bourgeois ideology."[12]

Evidence of this cleansing was uncovered by Mel and Norma Gabler in the early 1960's when they examined textbooks used by their children in government-run schools. According to

Robert W. Lee, the Gablers, "found so many examples of immorality, obscenity, socialism, and anti-Christian, anti-American bias that they decided to register a complaint with the Texas State Board of Education's Textbook Committee."[13]

And of course, the U.S. Supreme Court, along with the ACLU, has been working diligently to ensure that public schools in Soviet America are "cleansed" of all that is "religious," just as Foster had predicted.

So, the replacement of the American constitutional principle of "separation of church and state" with the Soviet constitutional principle of "separation of church and state" was predicted by the National Chairman of the Communist Party, USA in 1932 – exactly 30 years before the U.S. Supreme Court rendered it's 1962 ruling banishing prayer from our schools.

Foster added that, "...the dictatorship of the proletariat will produce a whole series of restrictions of liberty in the case of the oppressors, exploiters and capitalists."[14] One of those restrictions of liberty is the loss of the constitutionally protected right to the free exercise of religion by taxpayers on taxpayer-funded property!

Fact Number Thirty-Three:

Documentation of a Former FBI Agent

**A Former FBI Agent documented the
Communist plan to "Eliminate prayer or any phase of
religious expression in the schools on the grounds that it
violated the principle of 'separation of church and state.'"**

The goal of implanting the Soviet constitutional principle of "separation of church and state" within the United States was documented as "Current Communist Goal" Number 28 by former FBI agent W. Cleon Skousen. In the 1962 edition of his book, *The Naked Communist*, we find the following Communist goal: "Eliminate prayer or any phase of religious expression in the schools on the grounds that it violates the principle of 'separation of church and state.'"[15]

Are U.S. Supreme Court justices ignorant of this Communist plan, or are they deliberately ignoring it? If they are ignorant of this Communist plan, they lack the breadth of knowledge necessary to sit on the highest court in the land. If they are aware of this Communist plan and are deliberately ignoring it, then they lack the integrity to serve on the U.S. Supreme Court. In either case, they should be impeached and removed from the bench!

Fact Number Thirty-Four:

Documentation of a U.S. Congressman

A U.S. Congressman documented the Communist plan to "Eliminate prayer or any phase of religious expression in the schools on the grounds that it violates the principle of 'separation of church and state.'"

In 1963 U.S. Representative Albert Herlong, Jr., a conservative Democrat from the state of Florida, placed into the *U.S. Congressional Record* the complete list of the 45 "Current Communist Goals" outlined by former FBI agent W. Cleon

Skousen in his 1962 book, *The Naked Communist.* This act documented within the federal government the Communist origin of the principle of "separation of church and state" as now defined by the U.S. Supreme Court.[16]

Is the U.S. Supreme Court ignorant of the fact that this Communist goal has been entered into the *U.S. Congressional Record*, or is the Court deliberately ignoring this fact? What does this say about the U.S. Supreme Court and the decisions it makes regarding the advancement of this Communist goal?

Fact Number Thirty-Five:

The ACLU

A Communist founded the ACLU in 1920 to advance, among other goals, the Soviet constitutional principle of "separation of church and state"

One of the most ferocious organizations that seeks to enforce Communist Goal Number 28 and force the Soviet constitutional principle of "separation of church and state" upon the American people is the American Civil Liberties Union, or ACLU. This subversive organization was co-founded in 1920 by Roger Nash Baldwin, a self-pro-claimed supporter of communism who said,

"I am for Socialism, disarmament and ultimately, for the abolishing of the State itself...I seek the social ownership of property, the abolition of the propertied class and sole control of those who produce wealth. Communism is the goal."[17]

In 1931 a Special House Committee investigating Communist activities reported the following regarding the ACLU:

"The American Civil Liberties Union is closely affiliated with the communist movement in the United States, and fully 90 percent of its efforts are on behalf of communists who have come into conflict with the law. It claims to stand for free speech, free press and free assembly, but it is quite apparent that the main function of the ACLU is an attempt to protect the communists."[18]

One of the many co-founders of the ACLU was Helen Gurley Flynn, the first female Chairperson of the National Committee of the Communist Party, USA. She died while visiting the Soviet Union, and was given a state funeral by fellow Communists. The Communist Party, USA receives it's instructions from Moscow, Russia, just as the domestic Communist terrorist organization known as the Weather Underground, which was co-founded by Barack Obama's friend, William Ayers, received it instructions from Moscow, Russia which were transmitted through Havana, Cuba.

This, of course, explains why Barack Obama normalized relations with Communist Cuba while he was President, and instructed U.S. intelligence agencies to share intelligence with Communist Cuba. He did so supposedly to help fight against terrorism. However, as Obama knows, Communist Cuba is a state sponsor of terrorism! (Yes, truth is often stranger than fiction!)

ACLU co-founder Roger Baldwin visited the Soviet Union several times, and in 1927 he wrote *Liberty Under the Soviets*, wherein he praised the USSR – which President Ronald Reagan would later refer to as the "Evil Empire!" When Joseph Stalin signed a non-aggression pact with Adolf Hitler in 1939, Roger Baldwin denounced this act and expelled other Communists from the ACLU. After Roger Baldwin retired from the ACLU he maintained an office in the United Nations – an organization that was enthusiastically endorsed by homicidal, genocidal Communist dictators such as Joseph Stalin and Nikita Khrushchev. Baldwin died in 1981.[19]

One thing is certain, from its inception the ACLU has remained true to its Communist roots, even after Baldwin expelled other Communists. As Devvy Kidd[20] has written, the ACLU has been aggressively implementing the Communist agenda. According to Kidd, "For the past few decades, the ACLU has been on a major crusade to destroy Christianity in America," and also to "promote filth under 'freedom of speech and expression.'" From among the 45 Communist goals placed into the *U.S. Congressional Record* in 1963 by Representative Albert Herlong, Jr., Devvy Kidd stated that the ACLU has worked tirelessly to pursue a dozen Communist goals "in their quest to destroy America's culture and traditions."

At this point it is important to note that Democrat President Jimmy Carter awarded Roger Baldwin the Metal of Freedom on January 16, 1981 – four days before turning over the Office of the Presidency to Republican Ronald Reagan – a staunch anti-Communist! In addition, Democrat President Bill Clinton nominated Ruth Bader Ginsburg to the U.S. Supreme Court in 1993. Her nomination was approved 96 to 3 by the U.S. Senate. As a member of the U.S. Supreme Court Ginsburg supported the Soviet constitutional principle of "separation of church and state" when ruling on *Santa Fe Independent School District v. Doe*. Before Ruth Bader Ginsburg joined the Court, she served as a volunteer lawyer, Board member, and General Counsel to the ACLU. According to the *Chicago Tribune*,[21] Ruth Bader Ginsburg served as "the head of the American Civil Liberties Union's Women's Rights Project in the 1970s," and she "won several key Supreme Court cases to advance sexual equality."

Did Bill Clinton and the 93 members of the U.S. Senate know that Ruth Bader Ginsburg worked for an organization created by and staffed by Communists? Did they know that Congressman Albert Herlong, Jr. placed a list of 45 Communist goals into the *U.S. Congressional Record* which included the fraudulent imposition of the Soviet constitutional principle of "separation of church and state" upon the American people? Did they even care? Why are no mainstream "investigative journalists" asking these questions?

Fact Number Thirty-Six:

Judicial Temperament

**U.S. Supreme Court Justices who support the
Soviet constitutional principle of "separation
of church and state" lack the judicial temperament to
serve on the Court and uphold their second oath of office**

On April 10, 2017, Judge Neil Gorsuch was publicly sworn in as an Associate Justice to the U.S. Supreme Court. Associate Justice Anthony Kennedy administered the oath to Judge Gorsuch in the White House Rose Garden. But before doing so Justice Kennedy made a public statement which included the following:

"As many of you know, there are two oaths that a member of the judiciary takes. The first is the Constitutional Oath, which many of you are familiar with; it applies to all three branches of the government. The second oath is one that applies only to federal judges. Both of the oaths date from the founding of the republic. The judicial oath dates from 1789."

When Associate Justice Anthony Kennedy administered the second oath of office, Judge Neil Gorsuch said the following:

"I, Neil M. Gorsuch, do solemnly swear (or affirm) that I will administer justice without respect to persons, and do equal right to the poor and to the rich, and that I will faithfully and impartially discharge and perform all the duties incumbent upon me as Associate Justice of the Supreme Court of the United States, under the Constitution and laws of the United States. So help me God." (See Appendix F for the first and second oaths of office taken by U.S. Supreme Court Justices)

After taking the second oath of office, Associate Justice Neil Gorsuch delivered a brief speech wherein he promised "to be a faithful servant of the Constitution and the laws of this great nation."

As stated earlier, in the year 2000 the U.S. Supreme Court ruled in *Santa Fe Independent School District v. Doe* that student-led, student-initiated prayer before a football game was unconstitutional. However, William Rehnquist, Antonin Scalia, and Clarence Thomas, the three dissenting justices in this ruling, wrote that the majority opinion rendered by the other six justices "bristles with hostility to all things religious in public life."[22]

This observation is consistent with the conclusion drawn by President Ronald Reagan when he said, "...the frustrating thing is that those who are attacking religion claim they are doing it in the name of tolerance, freedom, and openmindedness. Question: Isn't the real truth that they are intolerant of religion? They refuse to tolerate its importance in our lives."[23] This overt emotional hostility towards religion rendered the six majority members of the U.S. Supreme Court incapable of formulating an objective decision, and they should have recused themselves from this case – and all similar cases.

Because the opinion of these six justices "bristles with hostility to all things religious in public life," they violated their second oaths of office wherein they swore or affirmed to "...faithfully and impartially discharge and perform all the duties incumbent upon" them as Associate Justices of the U.S. Supreme Court. One cannot be impartial regarding a religious court case while bristling with hostility to all things religious in public life.

The anti-religious hostility of the majority members of the U.S. Supreme Court is consistent with the anti-religious and anti-Christian hostility expressed in statements made by Communists such as Anatoly V. Lunarcharsky, the Russian Commissar of Education, who stated the following: "We hate Christians and Christianity. Even the best of them must be considered our worst enemies. Christian love is an obstacle to the development of the revolution. Down with love of one's neighbor! What we want is hate...Only then can we conquer the universe."[24]

Fact Number Thirty-Seven:

Violating Their First Oath of Office

**U.S. Supreme Court Justices who support the
Soviet constitutional principle of "separation of church
and state" are violating their first oath of office**

Before the public swearing in ceremony in the White House Rose Garden, Chief Justice John Roberts privately administered the below "Constitutional Oath" to Judge Neil Gorsuch:

"I, Neil M. Gorsuch, do solemnly swear (or affirm) that I will support and defend the Constitution of the United States against all enemies, foreign and domestic; that I will bear true faith and allegiance to the same; that I take this obligation freely, without any mental reservation or purpose of evasion; and that I will well and faithfully discharge the duties of the office on which I am about to enter. So help me God."

By replacing the American constitutional principle of "separation of church and state" with the Soviet constitutional principle of "separation of church and state," the U.S. Supreme Court justices violated their first oaths of office in at least two ways. Firstly, they swore to "support and defend the Constitution of the United States against all enemies, foreign and domestic." But instead of supporting and defending the U.S. Constitution against its enemies, they sided with those enemies. Secondly, by falsely portraying a Soviet constitutional principle as an American constitutional principle, they failed to "bear true faith and allegiance" to the U.S. Constitution. This leads us to Fact Number Thirty-Eight below!

Fact Number Thirty-Eight:

Article VI, Clause 2, of the U.S. Constitution

U.S. Supreme Court Justices who support the Soviet constitutional principle of "separation of church and state" are in violation of Article VI, Clause 2, of the U.S. Constitution

Article VI, Clause 2, of the U.S. Constitution states the following:

"**This Constitution**, and the Laws of the United States which shall be made in Pursuance thereof; and all Treaties made, or which shall be made, under the Authority of the United States, **shall be the supreme Law of the Land**; and the Judges in every State shall be bound thereby, any Thing in the Constitution or Laws of any State to the Contrary notwithstanding." (Bold lettering added)

So, regarding "separation of church and state," the U.S. Supreme Court has ruled that the Soviet Constitution, not the U.S. Constitution, is the "supreme law of the land." The Court has determined that they shall follow, and the American people shall be bound by, Article 52 of the Soviet Constitution, and not by Article VI, Clause 2, of the U.S. Constitution!

It's OK for the U.S. Supreme Court to "Think outside the box" when reviewing court cases; however, it is not OK for the U.S. Supreme Court to "Think outside the U.S. Constitution" when reviewing court cases. Each and every time they do so they violate both their first and second oaths of office!

Fact Number Thirty-Nine:

Justices Say a Short Prayer

**When sworn into office,
U.S. Supreme Court Justices say a
short prayer with their hand on a Bible
while on government property**

Recall that under Fact Number Eleven, it was noted that our Founding Fathers used the Bible on federal government property to conduct official government business, such as the swearing in of new presidents of the United States. It was further noted that this tradition was established by George Washington, our first President, and it continues to this day.

Likewise, it should be noted that when Associate Justice Anthony Kennedy swore in Neil Gorsuch as a new Associate Justice to the U.S. Supreme Court, Neil Gorsuch placed his hand on a Bible. Note further that the Bible was located in the Rose garden of the White House, which is federal government property.

It must be further noted that Neil Gorsuch, like all other newly appointed U.S. Supreme Court justices, ended his sworn statement with the words, "So help me God!" Recall the discussion of "So help me God" under Fact Number Eleven. Based on that discussion we could ask the same question we asked regarding George Washington when he ended his sworn statement with the words, "So help me God."

Who was Neil Gorsuch addressing when he said, "So help me God?" Clearly, like George Washington, he was addressing God. One may conclude that he was either asking God for help, which is a form of prayer, or affirming to God that he will faithfully execute his duties as a new Associate Justice, which is also a form of prayer! As stated earlier, both are instances wherein the oath-taker talks to God, which is the very definition of prayer! And Judge Neil Gorsuch said this publicly on federal government property – twice, once for each of the two oaths of office!

How can we have a U.S. Supreme Court Justice praying on federal government property when the U.S. Supreme Court says praying on federal government property is a violation of the U.S. Constitution? Keep in mind the fact that all members of the U.S. Supreme Court prayed on federal government property as they were sworn into office, including the U.S. Supreme Court justices who would later claim that such behavior was unconstitutional! So, they were violating the U.S. Constitution while they were swearing to defend the U.S. Constitution! This is just one of the many absurdities created by the U.S. Supreme Court when it repeatedly substituted the Soviet constitutional principle of "separation of church and state" for the U.S. Constitutional principle of "separation of church and state."

How can U.S. Supreme Court justices pray on government property and use the Bible on government property when the U.S. Supreme Court has ruled that prayer and the use of the Bible on government property is unconstitutional?

This is the **first of four examples** wherein the U.S. Supreme Court violated its own Soviet constitutional principle of "separation of church and state."

Fact Number Forty:

The Court and the Ten Commandments

**The U.S. Supreme Court concluded it is
unconstitutional to post the Ten Commandments
on government property, but the Ten Commandments
are posted on the U.S. Supreme Court Building,
which is government property**

As stated at the very beginning of this book, in 1980 the U.S. Supreme Court ruled in *Stone v. Graham* that it was unconstitutional for the Ten Commandments to be posted in a public school classroom. As a consequence of this decision the Ten Commandments have been forcibly removed from numerous government properties across the nation. However, while the U.S. Supreme Court ruled that is was unconstitutional to display the Ten Commandments on government property, we find that the Ten Commandments are displayed on the U.S. Supreme Court building, which is government property!²⁵

This is clearly another example of "Do as I say, but not as I do," which is a common practice among those who live by a double standard, one for them, the elite, and another for others, their subordinates, servants, and others considered to be "inferior!"

How can U.S. Supreme Court justices display the Ten Commandments on government property when the U.S. Supreme Court has ruled that displaying the Ten Commandments on government property is unconstitutional?

This is the **second example** of the U.S. Supreme Court violating its own Soviet constitutional principle of "separation of church and state."

Fact Number Forty-One:

The Court and a Funeral Service

All nine U.S. Supreme Court Justices attended a religious funeral service held in a church located on federal government property

Thurgood Marshall, a former U.S. Supreme Court Associate Justice, passed away in 1993. His funeral services were held at the Washington National Cathedral, and President William Jefferson Clinton attended the church services. In addition, all nine U.S. Supreme Court justices serving on the Court at that time attended the funeral services – which was a Christian religious service held in a church located on federal government property!

A 1993 *Los Angeles Times* headline read as follows: "Marshall Eulogized as 'Rock of Justice' Tribute: In services at Washington National Cathedral, former law clerks and friends recalled the jurist as a visionary who never gave up hope."[26]

How can U.S. Supreme Court justices attend religious services in a church located on government property when the U.S. Supreme Court has ruled that it is unconstitutional for religious services to be held on government property? (The Washington National Cathedral is discussed under Fact Number Forty-Seven)

This is the **third example** of the U.S. Supreme Court violating its own Soviet constitutional principle of "separation of church and state."

Fact Number Forty-Two:

Justices Allow a Short Prayer

The U.S. Supreme Court opens each session with a short prayer

This should be in "Ripley's Believe it or Not." The U.S. Supreme Court that concluded it is unconstitutional for prayer to occur on government property, opens each session with a prayer on government property. In addition, the prayer is initialed by a government employee who is paid with taxpayer dollars!

As stated at ACLJ.org, "...the Supreme Court of the United States starts each session with the phrase, God Save The United States and This Honorable Court. The statement is made by a Court Marshall, who is a federal employee."[27] Clearly, "God Save The United States and This Honorable Court" is an appeal to God, which is, by definition, a form of prayer. Unbelievable! How has the U.S. Supreme Court and its supporters gotten away with this obvious scam decade, after decade, after decade? Where are all the so-called investigative journalists?

How can U.S. Supreme Court justices allow themselves to be led in prayer on government property when they have ruled it is unconstitutional for students to be led in prayer on government property?

This is the **fourth example** of the U.S. Supreme Court violating its own Soviet constitutional principle of "separation of church and state."

Fact Number Forty-Three:

The U.S. Constitution and the Word "Lord"

The U.S. Constitution contains the word
"Lord," which is a clear violation of
the Soviet constitutional principle of
"separation of church and state"

It should be noted that the last paragraph of the U.S. Constitution states the following under Article VII: "Done in convention, by the unanimous consent of the states present, the 17th day of September, **in the year of our Lord 1787**, and of the independence of the United States of America the 12th. In Witness thereof we have hereunto subscribed our names." (Bold lettering added above and below)

Those who support the Soviet constitutional version of "separation of church and state" want to remove "In God We Trust" from our money; they want to remove "One Nation Under God" from the Pledge of Allegiance to the American Flag! If we do that, we must also remove "**in the year of our Lord 1787**" from the U.S. Constitution.

Such wording, "**in the year of our Lord 1787**," clearly violates the constitutional principle of "separation of church and state" as defined by the federal judiciary today! Therefore, according to the U.S. Supreme Court, **the U.S. Constitution must be declared unconstitutional**! The fact that the U.S. Constitution contains the words "**in the year of our Lord 1787**" demonstrates beyond all doubt that Court decisions regarding "separation of church and state" were, and remain, conspicuously illogical and therefore indefensible!

Because news, information, and education are dominated by people who do not understand the U.S. Constitution – or actually despise it and deliberately misrepresent it, most Americans are truly ignorant of the role of God and religion in the lives of our Founding Fathers. Most Americans do not know that most of the Founders of our government were deeply committed to their religious faith and the concept of religious liberty.

Fact Number Forty-Four:

The Constitutions of All 50 States

The Constitutions of all 50 states make reference to God in one form or another

You won't learn this in government-controlled schools; not at the elementary school level, high school level, or college level. You won't learn this from the so-called mainstream media. And you will seldom find this promoted by federal or state government officials. But nonetheless, every state constitution makes reference to God in one form or another. The constitutions of 43 states refer to God in the preamble. The other seven states make reference to God within the remainder of their constitutions.[28, 29]

According to Merriam-Webster.com, preamble is defined as "an introductory statement; *especially:* the introductory part of a constitution or statute that usually states the reasons for or intent of the law." So, although a preamble does not have the force of law as found elsewhere within a state constitution, it does provide a rationale for the provisions within the Constitution, and it documents the intent of the Framers of the Constitution. Let's review the preambles of constitutions from just a few states where the current leadership is decidedly secular or atheistic in their orientation today. (Note: for emphasis, bold lettering has been added to the state constitutions listed below)

In the Constitution of the State of California, which was ratified in 1879, we find the following preamble: "We, the People of the State of California, grateful to **Almighty God** for our freedom, in order to secure and perpetuate its blessings, do establish this Constitution."

The Constitution of the State of Hawaii, which was ratified in 1959, contains the following reference to a superior being: "We, the people of Hawaii, grateful for **Divine Guidance**..."

The Constitution of the State of Illinois, ratified in 1870, has the following reference to God: "We, the People of the State of Illinois – grateful to **Almighty God** for the civil, political and religious liberty which He has permitted us to enjoy and seeking His blessing upon our endeavors..."

In the Constitution of the State of Maryland, ratified in 1867, we find the following reference to God: "We, the people of the State of Maryland, grateful to **Almighty God** for our civil and religious liberty..."

The Constitution of the State of New York, ratified in 1938, contains the following: "We The People of the State of New York, grateful to **Almighty God** for our Freedom, in order to secure its blessings..."

As stated earlier, in Article VII of the U.S. Constitution we find the words, "**in the year of our Lord 1787.**" In addition, the words "**in the year of our Lord**" can be found in the constitutions of the following states: Arkansas, Colorado, Delaware, Iowa, Kentucky, Massachusetts, Nevada, New Jersey, Oklahoma, South Carolina, Tennessee, Utah, and Wyoming. In addition the words "**So help me God**," can be found in the constitutions of 20 states. (Bold lettering added above for emphasis)

Remember, in the 1947 case of *Everson v. Board of Education*, the U.S. Supreme Court ruled that the Bill of Rights in the U.S. Constitution applies to all 50 states; therefore, all 50 state governments must obey and enforce the Soviet constitutional principle of "separation of church and state."

For a detailed review of the 50 state constitutions and their references to God in one form or another, the reader is encouraged to visit the following two websites:

1. https://www.usconstitution.net/states_god.html

2. http://undergod.procon.org/view.resource.php?resourceI D=000081

Fact Number Forty-Five:

The National Day of Prayer

The Federal Government
promotes prayer through the
National Day of Prayer

The National Day of Prayer is rooted in America's Christian founding. As far back as 1775 the Continental Congress called for a time of prayer, and encouraged the colonies to pray for the birth of a new nation. In 1863 President Abraham Lincoln issued a proclamation calling for a day of "humiliation, fasting, and prayer." In 1952 both chambers of Congress passed a resolution calling for a National Day of Prayer. When it arrived on the desk of President Harry S. Truman, he signed it into law.

In 1988 Congress amended the resolution to establish the first Thursday in May of each year as the official National Day of Prayer. President Ronald Reagan signed it into law! Each year the President of the United States signs a proclamation to encourage Americans to pray on the National Day of Prayer. Recently all 50 state governors and the governors of several U.S. territories issued proclamations similar to that issued by the President. Although the National Day of Prayer was created by the federal government to encourage prayer across the entire nation, it is not an official federal holiday.[30, 31]

Why can the President promote prayer while on government property, but students and teachers are forbidden to promote prayer while on government property?

Fact Number Forty-Six:

The National Prayer Breakfast

The Federal Government
promotes prayer through the
National Prayer Breakfast

"The National Prayer Breakfast was started in 1953, when the Members of Congress invited President Eisenhower to join them for a fellowship breakfast, 'in the spirit of Jesus.'"[32] The National Prayer Breakfast is an annual event that occurs on the first Thursday of every February. Every U.S. President since Dwight D. Eisenhower has attended the National Prayer Breakfast since it began in 1953. This event is held in Washington, D.C., and most often takes place at the Washington Hilton's International Ballroom.

The National Prayer Breakfast is planned and executed each year by a Christian organization called the Fellowship Foundation. However, the event is hosted each year by members of the U.S. Congress. This event typically has two main speakers, the President of the United States and a surprise guest of significant notoriety.[33]

Clearly, the National Day of Prayer is an event where "separation of church and state" is inoperative as the President, Congressmen, and Christian leaders come to pray together on a yearly basis. Although this event is held in the Washington Hilton, this luxurious hotel is located in Washington, D.C., which is the capitol of the United States and under the exclusive control of the United States Congress! Washington, D.C. is the home of the President, Congress, and Supreme Court, and is a "federal district" as provided for in the U.S. Constitution.

Why can the President and Congress promote prayer while on government property, but students and teachers are forbidden to promote prayer while on government property?

Fact Number Forty-Seven:

The Washington National Cathedral

The U.S. Congress helped establish a church on federal government property in 1893 and continues its support to this day

In 1893 the United States Congress granted a charter (incorpora-tion papers) to the Protestant Episcopal Cathedral Foundation of the District of Columbia. This federal government issued charter authorized this Protestant Christian church to establish a cathedral and institutions of higher learning in the District of Columbia – which is federal government property. The end result of this federal charter was the construction of the Washington National Cathedral.

This federal charter was signed by President Benjamin Harrison, who served as the 23rd President of the United States (1889 – 1893); served as a colonel in the Union Army during the American Civil War, was a Presbyterian Church leader, and a Republican politician from the state of Indiana. This federal charter has been preserved in America's National Archives.[34]

According to History.com,[35] the Washington National Cathedral was originally conceived in 1791 by Major Pierre L'Enfant, who was commissioned by George Washington to design a plan to construct a capitol – or federal district – for the U.S. Government. This was the same year the Bill of Rights was ratified, and thus the same year the Establishment Clause of the First Amendment became operative. Construction of the Washington National Cathedral did not begin until September 29, 1907, and was not completed until 1990 – a span of 83 years!

As a fascinating footnote, construction began "when a stone from a field in Bethlehem was set into a larger slab of American granite and laid in ceremony as the foundation stone." The following biblical inscription was placed on the Bethlehem stone: "The Word was made flesh, and dwelt among us." (John 1:14). President Theodore Roosevelt was in attendance when the foundation was laid in 1907, and he spoke to a massive crowd.

Presidents Woodrow Wilson, Warren G. Harding, Calvin Coolidge, Franklin D. Roosevelt, Gerald R. Ford, and William J. Clinton attended various religious services at the Washington National Cathedral. In addition, President Woodrow Wilson is entombed in the Washington National Cathedral, and it hosted the state funerals of President's Dwight D. Eisenhower, Ronald Wilson Reagan, and Gerald R. Ford.[36, 37]

How can the U.S. Supreme Court allow the U.S. Congress to help establish a house of prayer and religious worship on government property when the Court has ruled that prayer and other religious activities on government property is unconstitutional?

Fact Number Forty-Eight:

National Prayer Services

**National Prayer Services are often
held at the Washington National Cathedral
which is located on federal government property**

In 1937 President Franklin D. Roosevelt attended a National Prayer Service for his second inauguration at the Washington National Cathedral. In 1985 the Washington National Cathedral hosted a national prayer service for President Ronald Wilson Reagan's second inauguration. In 1989 the Washington National Cathedral hosted a national prayer service for President George Herbert Walker Bush's inauguration. In 2001 the Washington National Cathedral hosted a National Day of Prayer and Remembrance Service a few days after the 9/11 terrorist attacks on American soil. All of these prayer services occurred in a church established by Congress, and which is located on federal government property.[38]

Fact Number Forty-Nine:

Reynolds v. United States (1878)

**Early American U.S. Supreme Court Justices
accurately concluded that Thomas Jefferson's
"wall" protected the church from the federal
government and not vice versa**

At WallBuilders.com[39] it is noted that a U.S. Supreme Court ruling prior to the 1947 *Everson v. Board of Education* case accurately concluded that Thomas Jefferson's "wall" protected the church from the state, and did not protect the state from the church. The case cited is *Reynolds v. United States (1878)*.

In this case, however, Jefferson's "wall" did not play a central role in the Court's ruling. It was, as Heritage.org[40] noted, orbiter dictum, meaning Jefferson's "wall" played an incidental or collateral role in the opinion of the justices. So, the case was not about "separation of church and state," but the principle was discussed by the justices. In their written opinion they provided the following:

"Coming as this does from an acknowledged leader of the advocates of the measure, it [Jefferson's letter] may be accepted almost as an authoritative declaration of the scope and effect of the Amendment thus secured. **Congress was deprived of all legislative power over mere [religious] opinion**, but was left free to reach actions which were in violation of social duties or subversive of good order." (Bold lettering added)

At WallBuilders.org it was further noted that, regarding Thomas Jefferson's employment of the words "separation between church and state," the Court concluded the following:

"[T]he rightful purposes of civil government are for its officers to interfere when principles break out into overt acts against peace and good order. In th[is]...is found the true distinction between what properly belongs to the church and what to the State."

In other words, the Court ruled that Jefferson's "wall" prohibited the government from interfering with religious activities, except when those activities violated various laws. Therefore, the government could interfere in religious activities that involved human sacrifice, incest, infanticide, and other horrific behaviors. This, of course, is simply commonsense!

Keep in mind that the supporters of the Soviet constitutional principle of "separation of church and state" may argue stare decisis, meaning that a precedent had been set in the 1947, 1962, 1963, 1980, 1992, and 2000 Court rulings. Therefore, with a long series of established precedents, the Court must continue to rule in a manner consist with previous rulings. However, precedent must be honored only when previous decisions have been rendered upon sound U.S. constitutional principles, and not upon Soviet constitutional principles. Furthermore, it may be argued by the opponents of the Soviet constitutional principle that a precedent was set in 1878, and that precedent was ignored in the 1947 ruling and subsequent rulings. In addition, in the 1983 ruling of *Marsh v. Chambers* the U.S. Supreme Court ignored the precedents set in 1947, 1962, 1963, and 1980.

As noted earlier, the U.S. Supreme Court has reversed itself partially or entirely more than 200 times in the past due to erroneous decisions. It's past time for the Court to reverse itself entirely once again!

Fact Number Fifty:

Dissenting Justices

Dissenting Justices in subsequent Court cases correctly concluded that Thomas Jefferson's "wall" protected the church from the federal government and not vice versa

The U.S. Supreme Court justices who have supported the Soviet constitutional principle of "separation of church and state" cannot claim ignorance as the basis for their misjudgments. They have been educated in face-to-face discussions with their fellow Court justices.

As stated under Fact Number Thirty-Five, in the year 2000 the U.S. Supreme Court ruled in *Santa Fe Independent School District v. Doe* that student-led, student-initiated prayer before a football game was unconstitutional. William Rehnquist, Antonin Scalia, and Clarence Thomas, the three dissenting justices in this ruling, wrote that the majority opinion rendered by the other six justices "bristles with hostility to all things religious in public life."

But not only did they exhibit hostility towards religious liberty in public life – as noted under Fact Number Thirty-Six; and not only did they ignore the precedent set by an earlier U.S. Supreme Court decision that accurately interpreted Thomas Jefferson's "wall," – as discussed under Fact Number Forty-Nine, they also ignored the correct conclusions drawn by their peers.

For example, in the **1962** case of *Engel v. Vitale* dissenting Justice Potter Stewart wrote: "With all respect, I think the Court has misapplied a great constitutional principle. I cannot see how an 'official religion' is established by letting those who want to say a prayer say it. On the contrary, I think that to deny the wish of these school children to join in reciting this prayer is to deny them the opportunity of sharing in the spiritual heritage of our Nation."[41]

In the **1980** case of *Stone v. Graham* Justice William Rehnquist wrote the following: "The Establishment Clause does not require that the public sector be insulated from all things which may have a religious significance or origin...Kentucky has decided to make students aware of this fact by demonstrating the secular impact of the Ten Commandments."[42]

In the **1992** ruling regarding *Lee v. Weisman*, Justice Antonin Scalia wrote: "Thus, while I have no quarrel with the Court's general proposition that the Establishment Clause 'guarantees that government may not coerce anyone to support or participate in religion or its exercise,' I see no warrant for expanding the concept of coercion beyond acts backed by threat of penalty – a brand of coercion that, happily, is readily discernible to those of us who have made a career of reading the disciples of Blackstone rather than of Freud."[43]

Finally, in the **2000** decision regarding *Santa Fe Independent School District v. Doe,* Chief Justice William Rehnquist wrote this eye-opening statement: "The Court distorts existing precedent to conclude that the school district's student-message program is invalid on its face under the Establishment Clause. But even more disturbing than its holding is the tone of the Court's opinion; it bristles with hostility to all things religious in public life. Neither the holding nor the tone of the opinion is faithful to the meaning of the Establishment Clause, when it is recalled that George Washington himself, at the request of the very Congress which passed the Bill of Rights, proclaimed a day or 'public thanksgiving and prayer, to be observed by acknowledging with grateful hearts the many and signal favors of Almighty God.'"[44]

Willful Blindness!

The Communist plan to "Eliminate prayer or any phase of religious expression in the schools on the grounds that it violates the principle of 'separation of church and state'" has been censored by the media, the education establishment, and nearly all U.S. government officials – including U.S. Supreme Court Justices

One can spend a lifetime listening to the radio, watching television, reading newspapers and magazines, attending high school and college classes on politics and law, and never learn about the Soviet constitutional principle of "separation of church and state." Americans who consider themselves to be well-informed and educated, never learned that, in 1963, U.S. Representative Albert Herlong, Jr. formally placed into the *U.S. Congressional Record* a complete list of 45 "Current Communist Goals," which included the Communist goal to "Eliminate prayer or any phase of religious expression in the schools on the grounds that it violates the principle of 'separation of church and state.'" As stated earlier, this act documented within the federal government the Communist origin of the principle of "separa-tion of church and state" as now defined by the U.S. Supreme Court.

Most "well-informed" and "educated" Americans have never heard of former FBI agent W. Cleon Skousen and his 1962 book, *The Naked Communist*, wherein the Communist goal of eliminating prayer or any phase of religious expression in the schools on the grounds that it violates the principle of "separation of church and state" was first introduced to the American public. Few Americans are aware of the 1932 book titled *Toward Soviet America*, authored by William Z. Foster, who was the National Chairman of the Communist Party, USA at the time of publication. Therefore, only a small minority of Americans are aware that in 1932 Fostered predicted that, in Soviet America, "God will be banished from the laboratories as well as from the schools," and in Soviet American schools, "The studies will be revolutionized, being cleansed of religious, patriotic and other features of the bourgeois ideology." Few Americans are aware of the book, *Welcome to Soviet America: Special Edition*, which reveals the alarming extent to which William Z. Foster's Soviet America has become a reality!

Any fair-minded person must ask, why is such critical informa-tion not openly discussed in government, the media, and academia? An in-depth examination of these Communist goals should be mandatory at every level of education in both public and private schools!

Chapter Four

The Johnson Amendment & The IRS

The Johnson Amendment is a provision in the U.S. tax code that prohibits all 501(c)(3) non-profit organizations, such as churches, from endorsing or opposing political candidates or political campaigns. However, according to Michelle Terry, "Our nation once had a longstanding tradition of church involvement in the political activity of the day. It was previously commonplace for pastors to preach about political issues and candidates."[1]

The Johnson Amendment was enacted into law as the Internal Revenue Code of 1954. It was proposed by Lyndon Baines Johnson when he was a U.S. Senator from Texas, and is thus called the Johnson Amendment. And, as Michelle Terry has stated, the Johnson Amendment was introduced by Democrat Senator Johnson to silence the voices of Texas non-profits that supported the political campaign of his opponent. Therefore, its passage was unrelated to concerns regarding "Jefferson's wall" or the principle of "separation of church and state." Its passage was politically motivated, and the Johnson Amendment was agreed to with little or no debate when placed in the Internal Revenue Code of 1954.

In recent years many Republicans, including President Donald Trump, have sought to repeal the Johnson Amendment, arguing that it restricts the free speech rights of churches and other religious groups. Repeal has been criticized because churches have fewer reporting requirements than other non-profit organizations, and because it would effectively make political contributions tax-deductible.

By prohibiting political speech the Johnson Amendment allows the federal government to breach Thomas Jefferson's "wall" and further trample the free speech rights of religious people!

Why can government people tell religious people what they can and cannot say on private religious property as a consequence of the Johnson Amendment, but religious people cannot tell government people what they can and cannot say on government property? Remember, the Bill of Rights, and thus the First Amendment, places restrictions on the federal government, not upon the American people.

As stated earlier, President Ronald Reagan rightly said our Founding Fathers created a Constitution that made the people the masters of government, and not vice versa!

Registering Churches

Churches in Communist China must register with the government, so why are churches in America registering with the government when such registration is unnecessary to achieve and maintain tax-exempt status?

Religious leaders who have registered their churches with the federal government as a 501(c)(3) fear they will jeopardize their tax exempt status if they engage in political activities. The IRS website states that a tax exempt 501(c)(3) organization "may not attempt to influence legislation as a substantial part of its activities and it may not participate in any campaign activity for or against political candidates."

However, at the Chalcedon.edu[2] website religious leaders learn from former IRS agents and tax attorneys that all churches automatically enjoy tax exempt status with the IRS whether or not they have registered as a 501(c)(3) organization. Some pastors have declined to register their churches with the federal government, knowing that such an act violates the U.S. constitutional principle of "separation of church and state" as described by Thomas Jefferson in his 1802 letter to the Danbury Baptist Association. They know beyond all doubt that Jefferson's "wall" prohibits the state from regulating or interfering with the religious activities of the church, and they behave accordingly. Many also know that registering churches with the government is what occurs in Communist China,[3] and therefore registration should not occur in a free America!

Religious leaders also learn at Chalcedon.edu that they can endlessly engage in issue advocacy while registered as a 501(c)(3) non-profit. Such speech by religious leaders is protected by the First Amendment to the U.S. Constitution. Quoting from a pamphlet issued by the Alliance Defending Freedom (previously called the Alliance Defense Fund, or ADF), we find the following:

"Issue advocacy, however, may not be limited by government and can be freely engaged in by churches. As long as one does not use explicit words expressly advocating the election or defeat of a clearly identified candidate, one is free to praise or criticize officials and candidates – this is called issue advocacy."[4] Also, there is no law that restricts churches from defining moral positions and asking people to vote accordingly.

According to the Alliance Defending Freedom,[5] "In *Taylor v. Commissioner of Internal Revenue*, the United States Tax Court agreed that, under section 508(c)(1) of the tax code churches do not have to apply for tax exempt status and are considered automatically exempt. But the court also stated, 'Nothing in section 508(c)(1) relieves a church from having to meet the requirements of section 501(c)(3).' Basically what the Taylor Court was saying is that churches are still subject to the restrictions in section 501(c)(3) of the tax code even if they never apply to the IRS for recognition of tax exempt status." According to the ADF, this is an unconstitutional restriction upon the free speech rights religious people.

Religious leaders must keep in mind *Ephesians 6:12*, wherein we find the following:

"For we wrestle not against flesh and blood, but against princi-palities, against powers, against the rulers of the darkness of this world, against spiritual wickedness in high places."

So, the Bible tells us that when we challenge corrupt flesh and blood politicians, bureaucrats, and U.S. Supreme Court justices, we are not fighting against them, but against the dark spiritual forces operating behind them. And it is most certainly the duty of every Christian to battle "against spiritual wickedness in high places." Does your pastor recognize this as his solemn duty?

Pastors played a leading role in the American Revolution, and perhaps God has put today's religious leaders in their current positions to lead His people in a revival to restore the Godly nation founded by our forefathers. Christian religious leaders must be guided by *2 Corinthians 3:17:* "Now the Lord is that Spirit; and where the Spirit of the Lord is, there is liberty." Conversely, when the Spirit of the Lord is absent, there is bondage, and we have been sliding into increasing levels of bondage for many generations.

It's time to reverse course! It's time for religious leaders to lead a movement to remove the Soviet constitutional principle of "separation of church and state" and reinstall the American constitutional principle of "separation of church and state."

President Trump Promised to Repeal the Johnson Amendment

"Why have we fought for 230 years to keep foreign governments from eviscerating our freedoms if we will voluntarily let our own government do so?" – Judge Andrew P. Napolitano[6]

At the National Prayer Breakfast on February 2, 2017, President Donald Trump stated the following: "My administration will do everything in its power to defend and protect religious liberty in our land." Mr. Trump added, "I will get rid of and totally destroy the Johnson Amendment."[7] The Johnson Amendment, as discussed in detail above, forbids churches and other 501(c)(3) nonprofit organizations from supporting political candidates or political campaigns.

On May 4, 2017, the day we observe the National Day of Prayer, President Donald Trump took the first step in keeping the promise he made at the National Prayer Breakfast three months earlier. According to CBN.com writer Jennifer Wishon,[8] on that day President Trump signed an executive order that accomplished three objectives: Firstly, it asserts that promotion and protection of religious liberty is a policy of the executive branch of the federal government. Secondly, it addresses the Johnson Amendment by instructing the IRS to employ maximum discretion when investigating tax-exempt organizations. Thirdly, President Trump's executive order provides regulatory relief to religious organizations (such as Little Sisters of the Poor) that oppose the morally objectionable contraception mandate foisted upon them by the Democrat Party under ObamaCare.

Jennifer Wishon further noted that President Trump's executive order "falls short of specifically addressing religious persecution in the military or that against individuals who practice their faith in all aspects of their lives, including the workplace." Also, what was illegal under the Johnson Amendment remains illegal, such as 501(C)(3) non-profit organizations endorsing political candidates and political campaigns.

As an author and public speaker, President Trump once said, "As long as you are going to be thinking anyway, think big."[9] So, let's think big and think beyond the Johnson Amendment. The U.S. Supreme Court's distortion of the principle of "separation of church and state" has restricted religious liberty to a far greater extent than the Johnson Amendment. As reported in the *Regent University Law Review* (Volume 24, 2011-2012, Number 2), when numerous pastors across America deliberately violated the Johnson Amendment beginning in 2008 and beyond, the IRS did not force the pastors to cease and desist.

Because the Soviet constitutional principle of "separation of church and state" is a much greater threat to religious liberty than the Johnson Amendment, we must encourage President Trump to challenge the U.S. Supreme Court's erroneous rulings on this critically important issue. By doing so President Trump would truly demonstrate that he is keeping the following promise: "My administration will do everything in its power to defend and protect religious liberty in our land."

Donald Trump may be the only President courageous enough to confront a corrupt U.S. Supreme Court and challenge the Soviet constitutional principle of "separation of church and state!" He is clearly one of the boldest and most outspoken American presidents since Teddy Roosevelt, the Rough Rider who became the 26th President of the United States in 1901. Because of his courageous military service, his big game hunting in Africa, his fight against government corruption, and his long, assorted public service career, we find the face of Teddy Roosevelt carved on Mount Rushmore alongside the faces of George Washington, Thomas Jefferson, and Abraham Lincoln. Like Donald Trump, he was a bold, unpredictable character who enjoyed celebrity status and a very accomplished life! And that, my friends, is precisely the type of character we need to challenge destructive decisions by a corrupt U.S. Supreme Court.

Steve Bannon, President Trump's former chief political strategist, stated at CPAC that the Trump Administration is on a mission to "deconstruct the administrative state."[10] According to AIM.org, President Donald Trump has asked Jerry Falwell, Jr., the President of Liberty University, "to head a White House task force on reforming the U.S. higher education system."[11] Cliff Kincaid of

AIM.org described this deconstruction task as *"Dismantling the Marxist Madrassas."*

In others words, President Trump plans to de-Sovietize William Z. Foster's Soviet America! The goal is to shrink or eliminate the corrupt, massive, intrusive, confiscatory Soviet-style bureau-cracies that have been established under previous presidents. By doing so President Trump would take a giant step toward reestablishing American-style freedom! That's why government officials, media personnel, and educators who support Soviet-style bureaucracies have become obstructionists – and why pro-Trump supporters face verbal and physical assault from the "dictatorship of the proletariat" when in public.

Of course, as President, Donald Trump cannot just sign an executive order and eliminate the Johnson Amendment; how-ever, he can inspire Congress to craft legislation that achieves that end! In addition, he cannot force the U.S. Supreme Court to reinstall the American constitutional principle of "separation of church and state" and abandon the Soviet constitutional principle. However, he can bring public attention to the twisted rulings rendered by the U.S. Supreme Court and begin a public campaign to reverse course.

Perhaps most importantly, he can work to ensure constitu-tionalists are placed on the high court when vacancies occur so that, at a future date, the past unconstitutional, destructive decisions of the Court can be corrected. Hopefully, the newly appointed U.S. Supreme Court Associate Justice Neil M. Gorsuch will follow in the footsteps of the late Associate Justice Antonin

Scalia – as he fills the vacancy created by Scalia's death in February of 2016.

Because President Trump faces fierce obstructionism from those who wish to stifle free speech among Bible-based Christians and Jews, "We the People" must encourage him and his inner circle to lead the way. This is supposed to be America, a Constitutional Republic, not North Korea, Communist China, or Communist Cuba – all of which are Marxist dictatorships!

Chapter Five

The Sinister Objective Behind
"Separation of Church and State"

Question:
**Why remove prayer, the Bible,
and the Ten Commandments from
the public sector based on the
Soviet constitutional principle of
"separation of church and state?"**

Answer:
**"Separation of church and state"
leads to separation of morality and state!**

Vladimir Lenin,[1] the Communist dictator who established communism in Russia and founded the Soviet Union gave his followers this advice: "Destroy a nation's morality, and it will fall in your lap like ripe fruit from a tree." This truism was recognized by Edmund Burke[2] who said, "Among a people generally corrupt, liberty cannot long exist." At Acton.org[3] we find the following: "Burke never separated religion and liberty; he maintained that liberty is only possible because it is part of the eternal and trans-cendent moral order."

Lenin, an enemy of liberty, and Burke, a lover of liberty, have both pointed out the fact that people who cannot control themselves via internal restrains, such as those found in the Ten

Commandments, will need external restrains to control them, thus justifying an authoritarian government with a police state.

Yes, the death of morality leads directly to the death of liberty! Just as imprisoned criminals lost their liberty due to their loss of morality, an entire nation can become a prison when deliberately overrun by government-manufactured street-level crime! In addition, a morally bankrupt electorate will elect morally bankrupt, predatory politicians whose number one goal is the imprisonment of their prey.

As stated earlier, in 1980 the U.S. Supreme Court ruled in *Stone v. Graham* that it was unconstitutional for the Ten Commandments to be posted in a public school classroom. With this decision the Court removed from our schools the Commandments, "Honor your father and your mother; You shall not steal; You shall not bear false witness against your neighbor;" and "You shall not murder." (Exodus 20:3-17.) By removing the Bible, prayer, and the Ten Commandments from government property, Communists and their supporters have worked to destroy America's morality so it would fall into their lap like ripe fruit from a tree, as taught by Communist Vladimir Lenin.

While the builders of William Z. Foster's Soviet America removed from our schools the Commandment, "Honor your father and your mother," they replaced it with questions such as the following that was asked in a "values clarification" class for third-graders: "How many of you ever wanted to beat up your parents?"[4] Also, the following question was asked in a fourth grade health class: "How many of you hate your parents?"[5]

Clearly, materials that encourage respect for parents were removed and replaced with materials that foster disrespect for parents. It should therefore come as no surprise that students are often instructed to not inform their parents about what they are taught in school,[6] and boards of education are given instructions on how to discredit parents who dare to complain about this and other forms of anti-parental brainwashing taking place in their children's taxpayer-funded re-education classes.[7]

In 1993 Thomas Sowell, a respected scholar and meticulous researcher, authored a book titled *Inside American Education: The Decline, The Deception, The Dogmas*.[8] In this book Thomas Sowell provided the reader with an in depth look at the deliberate damage inflicted upon the psyches of America's children in government-run schools. Most discouraging was the author's observation that, under "values clarification" our children are taught that "there is no right or wrong" way of thinking or behaving. In "death education," sex education, drug education, and "nuclear education" programs, children are psychologically conditioned to reject parental authority and parental values, and embrace nihilistic thought processes based upon the notion that there is no such thing as "right and wrong."

Through "values clarification" children are supposedly directed to clarify or better understand the values they embrace. However, as Thomas Sowell[9] has pointed out, values "confusion" would be a more accurate description of this brainwashing method. This conclusion is backed by reports of parents who testified before the U.S. Department of Education, with one parent stating that her son "came home one day very confused as to the rightness or wrongness of stealing" after being subjected to various psychological conditioning programs at school, including "values clarification."[10]

By employing techniques that ensure children are "confused as to the rightness or wrongness of stealing," "re-educators" deprogram our children of the Commandment, "You shall not steal," which was removed from government schools in 1980 by the U.S. Supreme Court. Clearly, through "values clarification" children are systematically deprogrammed of an important Commandment they may have learned at home or through religious training. They are cunningly deprogrammed of a principle that is necessary for the functioning of a self-governing individual and a low crime nation. And of course, when students are psychologically reprogrammed to believe that stealing is no longer viewed as wrong, they are prepared to accept, perhaps even demand, the implementation of socialism – which requires theft by government on a truly massive scale!

In his book *Why Johnny Can't Tell Right From Wrong: Moral Illiteracy and the Case for Character Education,* William Kilpatrick[11] discusses "values clarification" in some detail, but most disturbingly he reports that with this method, "teachers act like talk show hosts, and where the merits of wife swapping, cannibalism, and teaching children to masturbate are recommended topics for debate." Consistent with Thomas Sowell's contention that "values clarification" is a deceptive title for a program that leads to values confusion, Kilpatrick states that, "For students, it has meant wholesale confusion about moral values: learning to question values they have scarcely acquired, unlearning values taught at home, and concluding that questions of right and wrong are always merely subjective."

The successful moral destruction of America's school children can be summed up by the following 1993 observation made by William J. Bennett:[12] "In 1940 teachers identified the top problems in America's schools as: talking out of turn, chewing gum, making noise and running in the hall." Contrastingly, Bennett noted that, "In 1990, teachers listed drugs, alcohol, pregnancy, suicide, rape and assault" as the most pressing problems in America's schools. There is no better summary of the difference between the Bible-based traditional values America created by Washington, Jefferson, Adams, and Madison, and the Bible-free Soviet-style America created by the supporters of the Soviet constitutional principle of "separation of church and state."

This may be an appropriate place to cite some very disturbing figures regarding the destruction of morality among America's school children. This destruction is, in part, a consequence of the removal of prayer, the Bible, and the Ten Commandments from America's public schools and their replacement with "values clarification" and other leftist methods of indoctrination:

"...final FBI data from 1985-93 show that the number of adults age 25 or older committing murder decreased 20 percent. In the same period, homicides committed by 18- to 24-year-old males increased 65 percent. Homicides by 14- to 17-year-old males jumped 165 percent." – *The Arizona Republic,* May 22, 1995

"...8.8 percent of eighth and tenth grade students reported being robbed at school, 19 percent reported being threatened, and 9.5 percent said they were attacked." And, "...500,000 violent incidents occurred every month in public secondary schools in 1988." Also, "...57 percent of high school drug users said they bought their illegal substances at school." – William F. Jasper, *The New American,* August 8, 1994

"Moreover, 35 percent of juvenile inmates and 10 percent of students questioned believed it was 'OK to shoot a person if that is what it takes to get something you want.'" – "Violence climbing rapidly among America's young and ruthless," *The Arizona Republic,* September 8, 1995

Citing the 1982 book *The Disappearance of Childhood* by Neal Postman, William F. Jasper[13] points out that, "as recently as 1950 'in all of America, only 170 persons under the age of 15 were arrested for what the FBI calls serious crimes (such as murder, forcible rapes, robbery, and aggravated assault).'" However, "between 1950 and 1979 the rate of serious crime committed by children increased by 11,000 percent!" Yes, that's eleven thousand percent!

So, What Is Communism?

"The Communist world is a world of walls, searchlights, and guards – a prison for the heart, mind and soul." – J. Edgar Hoover, Director of the FBI, 1970[14]

Communism is Marxism adapted to Russia, China, etcetera; Nazism is Marxism adapted to Germany and Austria; Liberalism is Marxism adapted to America and the West!

What is communism? There are many definitions of communism, but in practice, communism is simply socialism with a police state – as defined by Pastor Ernie Sanders.[15] For that reason both socialism (which is the transfer of power from the private sector to the public sector) and a police state (which is the liberal use of law enforcement, backed by secret police) must be steadfastly discouraged. The extent to which socialism and a police state are advanced by those who are building a Soviet-style America, the more Communist-style oppression will be experienced by the American people.

Thus, Communist dictator Vladimir Lenin instructed his followers to destroy the morality of targeted nations because it would result in high rates of street crime, white collar crime, domestic violence, civil unrest, and other forms of manufactured crime, thus justifying the construction and maintenance of a police state. Hence the need to remove the prohibitions against murder, robbery, lying, respect for parents, etc. as found in the Bible and the Ten Commandments! If there is very little crime, there is very little need for a police state!

At this point the reader may ask, the American Left hates local law enforcement, so why would they want a police state? The answer is obvious for those who understand communism and Nazism: The builders of a Soviet-style America are working to render local law enforcement ineffective in order to justify centralized, federal control over all law enforcement, as seen under communism and Nazism!

In addition, it must be noted that criminals are uncomfortable living in a society with high moral values. They feel "oppressed" by people who tell them constantly that lying, cheating, stealing, and killing – as a way of life – are immoral behaviors and must be prohibited and punished. To people with criminal minds who have adopted the philosophy of the nihilist and the politics of the Marxist, lying, cheating, stealing, and killing – as a way of life – are viewed as normal, acceptable behaviors! Everybody does it! Hence, an electorate dominated by people with criminal minds will strive to elect like-minded people to positions of political power!

In terms of body count, Communists are the deadliest socio-paths to have ever walked the Earth! According to the late R. J. Rummel, a former professor emeritus at the University of Hawaii and author of the 1994 book, *Death By Government*, Soviet Communists murdered 61,911,000 men, women and children from 1917 to 1987. In addition, the Communist Chinese murdered 76,702,000 men, women and children during the 20th century. These figures are available for anyone to see at the University of Hawaii website displaying the work of the late R. J. Rummel.[16]

Keep in mind, these were victims who were hung, shot to death, worked to death in slave labor camps, starved to death, beaten to death, and tortured to death by their own government! The above numbers do not include victims of international wars, nor do they included victims of abortion. With a body count of 20,946,000 people, Nazi Adolf Hitler was an amateur compared to Communists Joseph Stalin, Mao Zedong, and their brethren.

William Z. Foster, National Chairman of the Communist Party, USA, wrote the following about his fellow American Commu-nists:

"With him the end justifies the means. Whether his tactics be 'legal' and 'moral,' or not, does not concern him, so long as they are effective. He knows that the laws as well as the current code of morals, are made by his mortal enemies... Consequently, he ignores them in so far as he is able and it suits his purposes. He proposes to develop, regardless of capitalist conceptions of 'legality,' 'fairness,' 'right,' etc., a greater power than his capitalist enemies have."[17]

The obvious, lawless substitution of the Soviet constitutional principle of "separation of church and state" for the American constitutional principle by the U.S. Supreme Court indicates that this judicial body is operating in a manner consistent with the above statement of Communist boss William Z. Foster, as well as his two other statements (published on 1932) listed below:

In Soviet America "God will be banished from the laboratories as well as from the schools."[18]

In Soviet American schools, "The studies will be revolutionized, being cleansed of religious, patriotic and other features of the bourgeois ideology."[19]

And of course, the Court's five decisions regarding "separation of church and state" are 100 percent consistent with "Current Communist Goal" Number 28 as documented in 1962 by former FBI agent W. Cleon Skousen in his book *The Naked Communist*, and recorded in the *U.S. Congressional Record* in 1963 by U.S. Representative Albert Herlong, Jr.: "Eliminate prayer or any phase of religious expression in the schools on the grounds that it violates the principle of 'separation of church and state.'"[20]

Chapter Six

Numerous Misjudgments by the U.S. Supreme Court have Fostered Widespread Hostility Towards Religious Liberty in The United States of America

If one investigates the number of situations across America wherein people have been forced to refrain from praying, forced to refrain from Bible reading, forced to refrain from displaying the Ten Commandments, forced to refrain from displaying Christian symbols, forced to refrain from displaying Christmas decorations, etc., since 1962, the number staggers the imagination!

For a mindboggling list of some of the crushing blows launched against religious liberty in the USA, the reader is strongly encouraged to download a free pdf of the following 66-page report: *Hostility To Religion: The Growing Threat to Religious Liberty in the United States,* June, 2017 Edition.[1] The report was compiled by the Family Research Council (FRC). According to Todd Starnes,[2] Tony Perkins, the President of FRC, said there has been a 76 percent increase in hostility toward religion in the United States in just three years – from 2014 to 2017. Perkins stated that "The recent spike in government driven religious hostility is sad, but not surprising, especially considering the Obama Administration's antagonism toward biblical Christianity."

He further stated that the FRC report justifies President Trump's stated plan to end policies within the federal government that "fan the flames of this religious intolerance." However, amidst the growing hostility towards religious liberty in this country, Perkins did report some good news regarding "the growing courage of Christians, especially young Christians, to defend both their faith and their freedoms."

Here is just a few of the disturbing titles found in the FRC report, which contains a seemingly endless list of attacks against religious liberty – much of which is a consequence of the U.S. Supreme Court's habitual misjudgments regarding the principle of "separation of church and state:"

ACLU Works to Stop Tourism Grant from Going to Christian Concert – November 2008

All Christmas Displays Banned from Washington State Capitol Building after Complaint from Freedom from Religion Foundation – October 2009

Freedom from Religion Foundation Attacks Mother Teresa Stamp – January 2010

Obama Administration Tries to Keep Prayer off World War II Memorial – November 2011

Government Bans Prayer at Homeless Shelter – July 2012

Atheist Group Demands Vietnam Veterans Memorial Be Removed – February 2013

Police Officers Forced to Resign Over Prison Ministry – May 2015

High School Class President Threatened with Arrest for Praying at Graduation – May 2011

Group [Freedom from Religion Foundation] Demands School Band Stop Playing God Bless America – August 2012

EEOC Investigates Firing of Teacher for Giving a Bible to a Student – January 2013

Pennsylvania School District Denies Equal Access to Religious Club – February 2013

Teacher Confiscates Student's Bible during Reading Time – April 2014

To review the entire list and read the stunning details contained in this FRC report, go to:

http://downloads.frc.org/EF/EF17F51.pdf

At the bottom of page one of the FRC report the reader finds the following:

"This report does not cover the many domestic religious freedom incidents that have occurred in the military context. For those, please see the Family Research Council report: "A Clear and Present Danger: The Threat to Religious Liberty in the Military, June 16, 2015 ed.,"[3]

Four Examples Of Taxpayers Who Have Been Punished as a Result of Numerous Misjudgments by the U.S. Supreme Court

Example Number One:

H.S. Football Coach Fired for Praying With His Team Players Files Lawsuit to Regain Employment

On October 17, 2015, Townhall.com[4] reported on a First Amendment, Establishment Clause case at Bremerton High School in the state of Washington. Joe Kennedy, the junior varsity football coach, prayed with his team members after each game for seven years. But Aaron Leavell, the Bremerton superintendant, wrote a letter to Coach Kennedy demanding that he stop praying with the team.

Based on the long series of misjudgments made by the U.S. Supreme Court, Aaron Leavell stated in his letter that Coach Kennedy's prayers violated the Establishment Clause of the First Amendment to the U.S. Constitution. Consequently, the free exercise of religious behavior exposed the school district to "significant risk of liability."

Although the ACLU was not mentioned, the decades-long pattern of lawsuits filed by the ACLU based on the misjudgments made by the Court has made many fearful of legal reprisals for taxpayers who engage in, or permit, the free exercise of religion on taxpayer-funded property.

Coach Kennedy disagreed with Superintendant Leavell, so he continued to pray with his team. As a consequence, Coach Kennedy was suspended, given a poor performance evaluation (the first one during his coaching career at Bremerton High School), and was eventually terminated.

In a follow-up article on August 9, 2016, Townhall.com[5] reported that Coach Kennedy did not walk away with his tail between his legs! He is fighting back!

Coach Joe Kennedy filed a lawsuit[6] against the Bremerton School District in the U.S. District Court, Western District of Washington at Tocoma. He is not seeking monetary compensation for wrongful termination; instead, he is simply asking to be reinstated as the junior varsity football coach at Bremerton High School.

According to Coach Kennedy's attorney, "Bremerton School District's actions violate Coach Kennedy's First Amendment rights to free speech and free exercise, as well as his rights under Title VII of the Civil Rights Act of 1964, which prohibits discrimination on the basis of religion."

In discussing this case with Todd Starnes, Franklin Graham said, "We have judges out there who hate God and hate His standards and disrespect the people who follow God."[7]

Example Number Two:

School Employee Threatened with Termination
if She Persists in Offering to Pray
for a Fellow School Employee

Ms. Toni Richardson[8] is a worker at Cony High School in Augusta, Maine. While working with a colleague she was concerned that he was not adapting well to his new job. In a meeting with supervisors Ms. Richardson stated that she "did not feel comfortable working with" her colleague because his classroom statements were "challenging" and "almost aggressive in the way they were delivered." She further stated that he "stood over" her, "pointed and used an aggressive tone." This behavior by her colleague caused "stress and discomfort" for Ms. Richardson.

Consequently, as a Christian who attended the same church as her colleague, she told him, "I will pray for you." She also reportedly said, "You were in my prayers." Keep in mind these were statements made by Ms. Richardson in a private conversa- tion with a fellow Christian. Unfortunately, the fellow Christian later complained about this behavior, and Ms. Richardson received a "coaching memorandum."

In the memorandum[9] the author cited the *Everson v. Board of Education* case wherein the U.S. Supreme Court ruled that the Establishment Clause of the First Amendment applied to the states as well as to the federal government. It was further noted that the Court concluded the principle of "separation of church and state" prohibited "public school-sponsored religious expres- sion." Therefore, Ms. Richardson was to refrain from integrating her "public and private belief systems when in the public schools" and further cease making reference to her "spiritual or religious beliefs."

Within the "coaching memorandum" it was stated that this memo did not constitute disciplinary action, but if there are further instances "deemed unprofessional by administration," she could face disciplinary action, and perhaps even dismissal.

Unbelievable! A Christian tells a fellow Christian she will pray for him, and she is told that further instances of this type of behavior could result in the termination of her employment. Keep in mind Ms. Richardson is not "guilty" of praying on taxpayer-funded property. She simply stated that she will pray for her colleague, and simply talking about prayer is perceived as a violation of a restriction that was placed on the U.S. Congress!

Yes, this is unbelievable! That is precisely why Ms. Richardson contacted the religious liberty law firm First Liberty Institute. Together with the Eaton Peabody law firm, they filed a formal complaint with the EEOC, or Equal Employment Opportunity Commission, "alleging religious discrimination and retaliation."

Example Number Three:

Sheriff Removes a Bible Verse
from Patrol Vehicles Fearing an
Expensive Law Suit from the ACLU

In May of 2017 Fox News reported that Sheriff C. H. Partin in Montgomery County, Virginia was forced to remove decals from county patrol vehicles which sported the following Bible verse: "Blessed are the peacemakers...Matthew 5:9."

The decision to remove the decals was made by the county Board of Supervisors. Sheriff Partin stated that a county supervisor informed him that, based on the legal advice they had received regarding this matter, "there are some serious concerns about the Establishment Clause and Separation of Church and State and the First Amendment." It was eventually concluded that removal of the decals was necessary because an attorney for the Montgomery County Board of Supervisors stated that "the decals would be a violation of the First Amendment based on the current case law because of the reference to Matthews 5:9."

Sheriff Partin stated that he had the decals placed on the vehicles in order to "honor our brothers and sisters in law enforcement." However, he removed the decals because "I don't believe the citizens of Montgomery County want me to get into a situation where hundreds of thousands of dollars of tax money may end up having to be given to the ACLU."[10, 11, 12]

Example Number Four:

A Federal Judge Bans Prayer at a
High School Graduation Ceremony
Thanks to a Single Student Protester
and the ACLU

An article in the *Chicago Tribune*[13] describes the banning of prayer at the Washington Community High School, in Washington, Illinois. With the help of the ACLU, a graduating student at the school, who claims to be a practicing Roman Catholic, convinced a federal judge to ban prayer at their graduation ceremony by issuing a temporary restraining order.

In the 80-year history of the school, this was the first occasion wherein the students, parents, and other audience members would not hear a prayer spoken at a graduation ceremony. In response to the court order, Ryan Brown, a graduating senior who was scheduled to speak, walked up to the gymnasium podium. Upon arrival "Brown paused, stepped to the side of the stage, folded his hands and bowed his head in a silent prayer. The gymnasium crowd of more than 1,000 students and adults erupted in cheers, with some standing to applaud while others blew air horns in celebration." In addition, Ryan Brown also faked a sneeze, which was prearranged with other students who then cried out, "God bless you!" To protest the federal judge's ruling, some students had "Let's Pray" and "Amen" taped on their caps. Others wore crosses around their necks.

It was reported that school officials had concluded the prayers were permissible because they were initiated by students, written by students, and would be spoken by students. However, as we have seen, in 1992 the U.S. Supreme Court ruled in *Lee v. Weisman* that it was unconstitutional for the state to sponsor prayer at school promotional activities and graduation cere-monies. And, in 2000 it ruled in *Santa Fe Independent School District v. Doe* that student-led, student-initiated prayer before a football game was unconstitutional in government schools.

Chapter Seven

It's Time to Impeach Corrupt Judges, including those sitting on the U.S. Supreme Court

"Constitutions have to be written on hearts, not just paper." – Margaret Thatcher, Prime Minister of the United Kingdom, 1979 – 1990[1]

Cliff Kincaid of Accuracy In Media (AIM)[2] has provided an excellent summary of a monumental book authored by the late attorney and activist, Phyllis Schlafly. Titled, *The Supremacists: The Tyranny of Judges and How to Stop It*, Schlafly provides constitutionalists with many options for ending what has accurately been deemed "Judicial Tyranny."

Cliff Kincaid clearly notes that the judges who have thwarted Donald Trump's efforts to prevent Islamo-fascist terrorists from entering our country are operating in violation of the U.S. Constitution and outside the law as written by the U.S. Congress. Restricting immigration on the basis of national security concerns is a duty of the executive branch of the federal government, not the judicial branch.

Just as judges ignore the undeniable facts surrounding the American constitutional principle of "separation of church and state," they also ignore the undeniable facts regarding the American constitutional principle of "separation of powers," as clearly outlined in the U.S. Constitution. By operating outside the U.S. Constitution and outside the law as written by Congress, such judges are not only a threat to the rule of law, they are also a threat to U.S. national security!

Therefore, I recommend that President Donald Trump have members of the U.S. Attorney General's office draft letters to outlaw judges whenever they are encountered. In the letters the lawless judges would be asked to specifically identify where in the U.S. Constitution the judicial branch of the federal govern- ment has been granted the authority to interfere with the constitutional duties of the executive branch.

In the letters the judges should find a warning that, if they are unable to adequately specify where in the U.S. Constitution they have been delegated the authority to usurp executive branch authority, then their unlawful rulings will be ignored. And if they persist in attempting to interfere with the duties of the execu- tive branch, usurp executive branch authority, and jeopardize U.S. national security, the President will ask Congress to initiate impeachment hearings against them.

In Chapter 15 of Schlafly's 2004 book, the President and Con- gress are provided with numerous tools to deal effectively with what should be called "Outlaw Judges." Cliff Kincaid provided the following summary of five useful tools based on the work of Phyllis Schlafly:

One: Reform Senate rules so liberals are not able to defeat constitutionalist nominees by preventing the Senate from voting them up or down.

Two: Curb the power of the judicial supremacists by legislating exceptions to court jurisdiction.

Three: Prohibit the spending of federal money to enforce obnoxious decisions handed down by judicial supremacists.

Four: Congress should impeach federal judges who make outrageous rulings that have no basis in the Constitution.

Five: Congress should prohibit federal courts from relying on foreign laws, administrative rules, or court decisions.

As previously noted in the Introduction, for those who believe it is impossible to impeach corrupt, lawless judges, they need to visit the website of the Federal Judicial Center.[3] At that site the reader finds a list of 15 federal judges who have been impeached by Congress. Of the 15 impeached federal judges, eight were convicted and removed from office; four were acquitted of the charges; and three resigned when faced with impeachment. So, 11 of the 15 impeached federal judges were removed from the bench. It has been done before! It should be done again!

For those who believe U.S. Supreme Court decisions cannot be reversed, they need to visit GPO.gov,[4] which lists more than 200 cases wherein the U.S. Supreme Court reversed itself partially or entirely. It has been done many times before, and it can be done again!

Cliff Kincaid also notes that at the Eagle Forum website established by Phyllis Schlafly, one can download a free digital copy of her book, *The Supremacists: The Tyranny of Judges and How to Stop It.* Each of the 15 chapters is downloaded separately, and they constitute a revised, 2006 edition of her book. Kincaid encourages Donald Trump's Cabinet and Congress to read Schlafly's book and arm themselves with the tools they need to put an end to the judicial tyranny of outlaw judges.

As stated earlier, Abraham Lincoln, our 16th President, gave the American people the following advice: "The people of these United States are the rightful masters of both Congresses and courts, not to overthrow the Constitution, but to overthrow the men who pervert the Constitution."[5] Clearly, the U.S. Supreme Court has repeatedly perverted the Constitution.

If you do not believe the Constitution has not been perverted, in addition to Phyllis Schlafly's book, *The Supremacists: The Tyranny of Judges and How to Stop It,* checkout the following three additional books: *The Constitution in Exile,* by Judge Andrew P. Napolitano; *Men In Black: How The Supreme Court Is Destroying America,* by Mark R. Levin; and *Who killed the Constitution?* by Thomas E. Woods, Jr. and Kevin R. C. Gutzman. The title, *Who Killed the Constitution,* tells us the U.S. Constitution is not only dead, but it did not die from natural causes. If the U.S. Constitution is dead, then the Constitutional Republic founded by George Washington, John Adams, Thomas Jefferson, and James Madison is also dead!

This conclusion is consistent with William Z. Foster's[6] contention that "The capitalist State [in America] must be broken down and the Workers' State built from the ground up on entirely different principles, and this was done in the USSR." This statement by Foster provides a solid clue to help us answer the question, *Who Killed the Constitution?* It also supplies us with a motive for the killing of the U.S. Constitution by outlaw judges!

Keep in mind that federal judges are nominated by the President and approved or rejected by the U.S. Senate. Therefore, corrupt judges are nominated by corrupt presidents and approved by corrupt senators. When Ron Paul[7] was a U.S. Representative he stated the following regarding his fellow politicians and their understanding of the U.S. Constitution: "...too many people in Washington – Republicans and Democrats – don't understand it and don't really believe in it, so they can hardly sell it." Former U.S. Representative Ron Paul therefore encouraged his fellow politicians to "read the Constitution and follow it."

As a libertarian Republican from Texas, Ron Paul stated, "I always tell my crowds that freedom is popular. The people still believe it." Wow! What further evidence do we need to conclude that, we have a Constitution, and we have a government, but we do not have a constitutional government! Ron Paul is also a physician, and while in Congress he had earned the nickname "Dr. No" because he routinely said "No" to proposed legislation which he deemed unconstitutional.

Chapter Eight

A Few Important, Final Thoughts

Denial, Delusion & Deceit

In the 1980s and early 1990s I spent about a dozen years working in an alcohol and other drug recover program located on Los Angeles' Skid Row. (Yes, Skid Row actually does exist!) As the program manager, I would try to walk through every area of the two-story program once each day to personally observe all staff operations, program participant activities, and the physical state of the facility.

On one occasion I walked into the laundry/shower area and found a male program participant preparing to "shoot up." He quickly gathered up his "kit" when he saw me. I told him that he would need to leave the program immediately because, as he surely knows, no drugs and no drug activity was permitted in an alcohol/drug recovery program.

To my astonishment, he denied that he was preparing to inject himself with an illicit drug. I was standing only a few feet away from him and his equipment, and he still made this denial. In effect, he was telling me that I did not see what I plainly saw with my own two eyes! He was denying an undeniable reality – and he expected me join him in his denial. Because of this behavior, he was forced to leave the program – drugs and all!

On another occasion an alcohol/drug counselor reported to me that he caught a male program volunteer behaving inappropriately with a female program participant. (The male program volunteer was reportedly a recovering alcoholic/drug addict, and the female program participant was in the initial stages of the recovery process.) When confronted by the counselor the volunteer denied the undeniable. He denied behaving inappropriately in spite of the fact that he had been caught "red handed" doing so. Although he claimed to be recovering, his behavior suggested he may still be practicing! He, too, was forced to leave the program.

When leftist judges, attorneys, law professors, politicians, and so-called journalists and civil rights activists tell us the U.S. Constitution does not mean what it says, occasionally I recall my experiences on Skid Row. I ask myself, how can people with law degrees deny what is plainly printed in black and white for anyone to read? How can they publicly state that the Establishment Clause does not mean what it says? How can they expect clear-thinking Americans to believe that the Establishment Clause of the First Amendment can contradict both the Free Exercise Clause and the Freedom of Speech Clause?

How can leftists tell us Thomas Jefferson believed it was unconstitutional for people to pray on government property when Thomas Jefferson prayed on government property? How can leftists tell us Thomas Jefferson believed it was unconstitutional for people to read the Bible on government property when Thomas Jefferson encouraged the reading of the Bible on government property? How can leftists tell us Thomas Jefferson believed it was unconstitutional for teachers to pray with their students on government property when Thomas Jefferson encouraged professors to pray with their students on government property?

The conclusion is obvious: the denial of reality by leftist judges, attorneys, law professors, politicians, and so-called journalists and civil rights activists is akin to the denial of reality by practicing alcoholics and other drug addicts. What is most disturbing is the fact that these reality-divorced individuals are forcing clear-thinking people to conform to their artificially created world – a world based on denial, delusion, and deceit!

It's past time to force these destructive individuals to leave the government, the media, and academia – because the denial of the American constitutional principle of "separation of church and state" and its replacement with the Soviet constitutional principle represents just one of countless examples where "We the People" are forced to relinquish our constitutionally-protected rights to leftists in positions of enormous power and influence who think and act like practicing, reality-denying, Skid Row alcoholics, crackheads, and heroin addicts!

To Leftists, The World is a Rorschach Test

On June 21, 2017, radio talk show host and author Larry Elder made the following comment on his radio program: "Republicans believe what they see; Democrats see what they believe!" This is consistent with an observation made by attorney Jonathan Turley.[1] When writing about the leftist media and leftist lawyers' obsession with possible collusion between the Trump team and the Russians, Jonathan Turley mentioned the Rorschach test used by psychologists to evaluate the mental health of individuals.

During the Rorschach testing session, individuals are provided with a series of cards containing simulated inkblots. Of course, each inkblot is simply that, a meaningless inkblot. When asked what they see when viewing the inkblots, the individuals being tested project their own meaning onto the simulated blots of ink. What is projected, of course, is a series of fantasies subjectively created by the individuals being tested. The pattern of projections reported by the individuals being tested reveals their fears, fantasies, motivations, and other inner thought processes. Test results may help reveal how an individual views the world!

This, according to Jonathan Turley, is precisely the psychological operation that occurs within the leftist media and many leftist legal commentators when they view the behavior of Trump and Trump team members. Turley said Trump, Jr. and others fell for a classic "bait and switch" operation when they met with a Russian attorney, but leftists projected their own meanings onto the meeting:

"While the participants have said that the meeting lasted only about 20 minutes and that the lawyer offered nothing in terms of such evidence – and instead pivoted to a discussion of rescinding a ban on Russian adoptions – the media went into a frenzy as experts spotted images of crimes from treason to defrauding the United States to campaign finance violations."

So, whether they are sitting in a newsroom or sitting on the U.S. Supreme Court, to leftists the entire world is a Rorschach test wherein, as Larry Elder has noted, they see what they believe when they should believe what they see! Alan Dershowitz agrees with Larry Elder and Jonathan Turley that liberals see things that do not exist!

Alan Dershowitz,[2] a Harvard law professor who supported Democrat Hillary Clinton, not Republican Donald Trump, in the 2016 presidential election, was interviewed by Jeanine Pirro of the Fox News Network to discuss leftist charges of collusion and treason against the Trump team. During their discussion Professor Dershowitz said, "I'm shocked as a civil libertarian, and a criminal lawyer and a liberal at how liberals are, some of them at least, prepared to stretch existing laws, talk about treason, talk about other kinds of crimes that just don't exist when it comes to the facts as we know them about this meeting...So I'm going to keep insisting we stop accusing people of crime when there is no evidence of crime."

Professor Dershowitz later added, "Collusion is not a crime unless it's committing a criminal act. But the treason thing upsets me...It is only, basically waging war against the United States...It's inconceivable that anybody with knowledge of the Constitution or American history would argue a private citizen, by securing information for a campaign,...has committed treason..." He further stated that, "We are miseducating [the] American people. We are miseducating young people."

It appears Professor Dershowitz may be a "Classical" liberal, which is a lover of liberty for all, not a "Contemporary" liberal, which is a lover of liberty only for those who agree with them. Classical liberals have a libertarian orientation, while contemporary liberals have fascist and Marxist orientations.

Leftists will say that the U.S. Constitution is a "living" document; therefore, we must interpret it within the context of the current culture, and not in a manner consistent with the original intent of the Framers. But the Constitution is a "living" document only to the extent that it can be altered through the amendment process. To simply say the justices on the Court can ignore the intent of the Framers is the equivalent of "fundamentally transforming" the U.S. Constitution into another series of inkblots upon which leftists can project their own personal biases, fears, and fantasies!

Perhaps this explains why leftists can see a man who looks like Ernest Borgnine and claim they see a woman, or why they can see a woman who looks like Marilyn Monroe and claim they see a man! To these DNA deniers, people are just like the U.S. Constitution, all of which are just another set of amorphous inkblots upon which they can project any desirable meaning!

An Example of Obvious Judicial Deceit

During U.S. Senate confirmation hearings U.S. Supreme Court nominees are asked many questions. Those questions tend to center around hot-button issues over which the Left and the Right continue to fight. So, nominees are usually asked to express their opinions regarding abortion and gun control. However, they are seldom or never asked to comment about the principle of "separation of church and state." The absence of such questions indicates that the supporters of the Soviet constitutional principle have won that argument, and senators on the political Right have surrendered on this most important issue.

Because U.S. Supreme Court nominees are always asked about gun control and the Second Amendment, it is this issue, and not Jefferson's "wall," where we are likely to find deceitful responses from nominees. Let's take a look at Judge Sonia Sotomayor's answers regarding the Second Amendment during her Senate confirmation hearings and compare them to her behavior after she was confirmed by the Senate.

In the case of *McDonald V. Chicago (2010)*, the U.S. Supreme Court ruled 5-4 that the right of an individual to keep and bear arms as protected by the Second Amendment is incorporated by the Due Process Clause of the Fourteenth Amendment. Therefore, just as states and cities must honor U.S. Supreme Court rulings regarding the principle of "separation of church and state," they must also honor Court rulings regarding the right to keep and bear arms.

In this decision Associate Justices Sonia Sotomayor and Ruth Bader Ginsburg joined the dissent of Associate Justice Stephan Breyer, who concluded that the Second Amendment did not protect the right of the people of Chicago to keep and bear arms, nor did it protect the right of any individuals in America to keep and bear arms. He thus argued that *District of Columbia v. Heller (2008)* must be reversed, and stated that, "In sum, the Framers did not write the Second Amendment in order to protect a private right of armed self-defense."[3]

As a former General Counsel to the Communist-created ACLU, one would expect Ruth Bader Ginsburg to support Soviet-style disarmament of our nation's citizens. But Sonia Sotomayor, who also joined with Stephan Breyer, stated the following in her U.S. Senate confirmation hearings: "I understand the individual right fully that the Supreme Court recognized in Heller." She also stated that, "I understand how important the right to bear arms is to many, many Americans."

So, when questioned during her U.S. Senate confirmation hearings, Sonia Sotomayor led the senators to believe that she recognized the Second Amendment protects the individual right of the people to keep and bear arms. However, once confirmed by the U.S. Senate and sitting on the U.S. Supreme Court as an Associate Justice, Sotomayor did a 180 degree turnaround and supported a dissent by Stephen Breyer that stated the Second Amendment did not protect an individual right of the people to keep and bear arms! (Keep in mind the Bill of Rights does not create rights nor does it grant rights, it simply protects the pre-existing, natural, God-given, inalienable rights of the people.)

So, Associate Justice Sotomayor sees what she wants to see in the U.S. Constitution – and she says whatever she needs to say in order to deceive others about her true intentions! She was nominated by President Barack Obama, who is no friend of the Second Amendment, nor is he a friend of most of the principles found in the U.S. Constitution.

It is most interesting that corrupt U.S. Supreme Court justices have selectively enshrined just a few (misjudged) words of Thomas Jefferson regarding the First Amendment, but they have ignored the following large amount of well-documented words of Thomas Jefferson[4] regarding the Second Amendment:

"Laws that forbid the carrying of arms...disarm only those who are neither inclined nor determined to commit crimes...Such laws make things worse for the assaulted and better for the assailants; they serve rather to encourage than to prevent homicides, for an unarmed man may be attacked with greater confidence than an armed man." – Thomas Jefferson, *Commonplace Book*, quoting criminologist Casare Beccaria, author of *On Crimes and Punishment*, 1764

"No free man shall ever be debarred the use of arms."
– Thomas Jefferson, Virginia Constitution, Draft 1, 1776

"A strong body makes the mind strong. As to the species of exercises, I advise the gun. While this gives moderate exercise to the body, it gives boldness, enterprise and independence to the mind. Games played with the ball, and others of that nature, are too violent for the body and stamp no character on the mind. Let your gun therefore be your constant companion of your walks – Thomas Jefferson, letter to Peter Carr, August 19, 1785

"What country can preserve its liberties if their rulers are not warned from time to time that their people preserve the spirit of resistance? Let them take arms!" – Thomas Jefferson, letter to James Madison, December 20, 1787

"The constitutions of most states assert that all power is inherent in the people; that they may exercise it by themselves...that it is their right and duty to be at all times armed..." – Thomas Jefferson, letter to John Cartwright, June 5, 1824

There is also a Biblical Explanation for the Lawlessness of Many Court Justices

"The coming of the lawless one by the activity of Satan will be with all power and with pretended signs and wonders, and with all wicked deception for those who are to perish, because they refused to love the Truth and so be saved. Therefore, God sends upon them a strong delusion, to make them believe what is false, so that all may be condemned who did not believe the Truth but had pleasure in unrighteousness." – 2 Thessalonians 2: 9-12

Concluding Statement

In light of the writings of Communist William Z. Foster, former FBI agent W. Cleon Skousen, FBI Director J. Edgar Hoover, and others, it is clear that the current culture war is, in reality, the Cold War being fought – and lost – on American soil. As the Greek writer and poet Aeschylus[5] wrote about 400 years before Christ was born, "In war, truth is the first casualty."

Consequently, the battle over the principle of "separation of church and state" is just one of many battles in a long-term culture war where truth is an obvious casualty on a daily basis. And it is on a near daily basis that President Donald Trump criticizes leftist news sources for their seemingly endless display of "fake news!" Clearly, leftists are culture warriors, but they are fighting against American culture. They are inundating us with denial, delusion, and deceit in order to create confusion, chaos, and violence, thus justifying the creation and maintenance of socialism with a police state!

Appendix A

Danbury Baptist Association
Letter to Thomas Jefferson

The address of the Danbury Baptist Association in the State of Connecticut, assembled October 7, 1801.

To Thomas Jefferson, Esq., President of the United States of America

Sir,

Among the many millions in America and Europe who rejoice in your election to office, we embrace the first opportunity which we have enjoyed in our collective capacity, since your inauguration, to express our great satisfaction in your appointment to the Chief Magistracy in the United States. And though the mode of expression may be less courtly and pompous than what many others clothe their addresses with, we beg you, sir, to believe, that none is more sincere.

Our sentiments are uniformly on the side of religious liberty: that Religion is at all times and places a matter between God and individuals, that no man ought to suffer in name, person, or effects on account of his religious opinions, [and] that the legitimate power of civil government extends no further than to punish the man who works ill to his neighbor. But sir, our Constitution of government is not specific. Our ancient charter, together with the laws made coincident therewith, were adapted as the basis of our government at the time of our revolution. And such has been our laws and usages, and such still are, [so] that Religion is considered as the first object of Legislation, and therefore what religious privileges we enjoy (as a minor part of the State) we enjoy as favors granted, and not as inalienable rights. And these favors we receive at the expense of such degrading acknowledgments, as are inconsistent with the rights of freemen. It is not to be wondered at therefore, if those who seek after power and gain, under the pretense of government and Religion, should reproach their fellow men, [or] should reproach their Chief Magistrate, as an enemy of religion, law, and good order, because he will not, dares not, the prerogative of Jehovah and make laws to govern the Kingdom of Christ.

Sir, we are sensible that the President of the United States is not the National Legislator and also sensible that the national government cannot destroy the laws of each State, but our hopes are strong that the sentiment of our beloved President, which have had such genial effect already, like the radiant beams of the sun, will shine and prevail through all these States – and all the world – until hierarchy and tyranny be destroyed from the earth. Sir, when we reflect on your past services, and see a glow of philanthropy and goodwill shining forth in a course of more than thirty years, we have reason to believe that America's God has raised you up to fill the Chair of State out of that goodwill which he bears to the millions which you preside over. May God strengthen you for the arduous task which providence and the voice of the people have called you – to sustain and support you and your Administration against all the pre-determined opposition of those who wish to rise to wealth and importance on the poverty and subjection of the people.

And may the Lord preserve you safe from every evil and bring you at last to his Heavenly Kingdom through Jesus Christ our Glorious Mediator.

Signed in behalf of the Association,

Neh,h Dodge }

Eph'm Robbins } The Committee

Stephen S. Nelson }

Source:

https://wallbuilders.com/letters-danbury-baptists-thomas-jefferson/

Appendix B

Thomas Jefferson's Reply to the Danbury Baptist Association

Messrs. Nehemiah Dodge, Ephraim Robbins, and Stephen S. Nelson, A Committee of the Danbury Baptist Association, in the State of Connecticut.

Washington, January 1, 1802

Gentlemen, – The affectionate sentiment of esteem and appro-bation which you are so good as to express towards me, on behalf of the Danbury Baptist Association, give me the highest satisfaction. My duties dictate a faithful and zealous pursuit of the interests of my constituents, and in proportion as they are persuaded of my fidelity to those duties, the discharge of them becomes more and more pleasing.

Believing with you that religion is a matter which lies solely between man and his God, that he owes account to none other for his faith or his worship, that the legislative powers of government reach actions only, and not opinions, I contemplate with sovereign reverence that act of the whole American people which declared that their legislature would "make no law respecting an establishment of religion, or prohibiting the free exercise thereof," thus building a wall of separation between Church and State. Adhering to this expression of the supreme will of the nation in behalf of the rights of conscience, I shall see with sincere satisfaction the progress of those sentiments which tend to restore to man all his natural rights, convinced he has no natural right in opposition to his social duties.

I reciprocate your kind prayers for the protection and blessing of the common Father and Creator of man, and tender you for yourselves and your religious association, assurances of my high respect and esteem.

Th Jefferson

Jan. 1. 1802

Source:

https://wallbuilders.com/letters-danbury-baptists-thomas-jefferson/

Appendix C

Constitution of the
United States of America

Article III

Section One

The judicial power of the United States, shall be vested in one Supreme Court, and in such inferior courts as the Congress may from time to time ordain and establish. The judges, both of the supreme and inferior courts, shall hold their offices during good behavior, and shall, at stated times, receive for their services, a compensation, which shall not be diminished during their continuance in office.

Section Two

The judicial power shall extend to all cases, in law and equity, arising under this Constitution, the laws of the United States, and treaties made, or which shall be made, under their authority; – to all cases affecting ambassadors, other public ministers and consuls; – to all cases of admiralty and maritime Jurisdiction; – to controversies to which the United States shall be a party; – to controversies between two or more states; – between a state and citizens of another state; – between citizens of different states; – between citizens of the same state claiming lands under grants of different states, and between a state, or the citizens thereof, and foreign states, citizens or subjects.

In all cases affecting ambassadors, other public ministers and consuls, and those in which a state shall be party, the Supreme Court shall have original jurisdiction. In all the other cases before mentioned, the Supreme Court shall have appellate jurisdiction, both as to law and fact, with such exceptions, and under such regulations as the Congress shall make.

The trial of all crimes, except in cases of impeachment; shall be by Jury; and such trial shall be held in the state where the said crimes shall have been committed; but when not committed within any state, the trial shall be at such place or places as the Congress may by law have directed.

Section Three

Treason against the United States, shall consist only in levying war against them, or in adhering to their enemies, giving them aid and comfort. No person shall be convicted of treason unless on the testimony of two witnesses to the same overt act, or on confession in open court.

The Congress shall have power to declare the punishment of treason, but no attainder of treason shall work corruption of blood, or forfeiture except during the life of the person attainted.

Source:

https://www.archives.gov/founding-docs/constitution-transcript

Appendix D

Constitution of the
United States of America

The Bill of Rights

Adopted 1791

Amendment I

Congress shall make no law respecting an establishment of religion, or prohibiting the free exercise thereof; or abridging the freedom of speech or of the press; or the right of the people peaceably to assemble, and to petition the government for a redress of grievances.

Amendment II

A well regulated militia, being necessary to the security of a free state, the right of the people to keep and bear arms, shall not be infringed.

Amendment III

No soldier shall, in time of peace, be quartered in any house, without the consent of the owner, nor in time of war, but in a manner to be prescribed by law.

Amendment IV

The right of the people to be secure in their persons, houses, papers, and effects, against unreasonable searches and seizures, shall not be violated, and no warrants shall issue, but upon probable cause, supported by oath or affirmation, and particularly describing the place to be searched, and the persons or things to be seized.

Amendment V

No person shall be held to answer for a capital, or otherwise infamous crime, unless on a presentment or indictment of a grand jury, except in cases arising in the land or naval forces, or in the militia, when in actual service in time of war or public danger; nor shall any person be subject, for the same offense, to be twice put in jeopardy of life or limb; nor shall be compelled, in any criminal case, to be a witness against himself, nor be deprived of life, liberty, or property, without due process of law; nor shall private property be taken for public use, without just compensation.

Amendment VI

In all criminal prosecutions the accused shall enjoy the right to a speedy and public trial, by an impartial jury of the State and district wherein the crime shall have been committed, which district shall have been previously ascertained by law, and to be informed of the nature and cause of the accusation; to be confronted with the witnesses against him; to have compulsory process for obtaining witnesses in his favor, and to have the Assistance of Counsel for his defense.

Amendment VII

In suits at common law, where the value in controversy shall exceed twenty dollars, the right of trial by jury shall be preserved, and no fact tried by a jury shall be otherwise reexamined in any court of the United States, than according to the rules of the common law.

Amendment VIII

Excessive bail shall not be required, nor excessive fines imposed, nor cruel and unusual punishments inflicted.

Amendment IX

The enumeration in the Constitution, of certain rights, shall not be construed to deny or disparage others retained by the people.

Amendment X

The powers not delegated to the United States by the Constitution, nor prohibited by it to the States, are reserved to the States respectively or to the people.

Source:

http://avalon.law.yale.edu/18th_century/rights1.asp

Appendix E

Separation of Church and State in the Soviet and Russian Constitutions

The principle of "separation of church and state" could not be found in the 1924 USSR Constitution, but was located in the 1936 USSR Constitution, which some people refer to as the "Stalin" Constitution. So, it was under the leadership of Communist mass murderer Joseph Stalin that the principle of "separation of church and state" was introduced into the Soviet Constitution. This principle was later placed in Article 52 of the 1977 Soviet Constitution and also in Article 14 of the Russian Federation's Constitution of 1993.

Constitution of the USSR

Adopted 1936

Chapter 10:

Fundamental Rights and Duties of Citizens

Article 124

In order to ensure to citizens freedom of conscience, the church in the U.S.S.R. is separated from the state, and the school from the church. Freedom of religious worship and freedom of anti-religious propaganda is recognized for all citizens.

Sources:

The Text of the Constitution of the USSR 1924;
Constitution of the Union of Soviet Socialist Republics

http://constitution.sokolniki.com/eng/History/RussianConstitutio
ns/10266.aspx

1936 Constitution of the USSR

http://www.departments.bucknell.edu/russian/const/1936toc.htm
l

Constitution
(Fundamental Law)

The Union of Soviet Socialist Republics

Adopted October 7, 1977

II. The State and the Individual

Chapter 7:

The Basic Rights, Freedoms,
and Duties of Citizens of the USSR

Citizens of the USSR are guaranteed freedom of conscience, that
is, the right to profess or not to profess any religion, and to

conduct religious worship or atheistic propaganda. Incitement of hostility or hatred on religious grounds is prohibited. In the USSR, the church is separated from the state, and the school from the church.

Source:

http://www.departments.bucknell.edu/russian/const/77cons02.html#chap07

Russian Federation's Constitution
of 1993 with Amendments through 2008

Article 14

1. The Russian Federation shall be a secular state. No religion may be established as the State religion or as obligatory.

2. Religious associations shall be separate from the State and shall be equal before the law.

The Russian constitutional statement, "No religion may be established as the State religion or as obligatory" is consistent with America's Founding Father's understanding of "separation of church and state" as expressed in the U.S. Constitution. It is certainly consistent with Thomas Jefferson's statements and behavior regarding the relationship between church and state. So, in part one of Article 14 the Russians have a very clear "Establishment Clause" in their 1993 Constitution. However, in part two under of Article 14 we find a clear "separation of religion and state" that is consistent with Article 124 of the 1936 Soviet Constitution and with Article 52 of the 1977 Soviet Constitution.

Source:

https://www.constituteproject.org/constitution/Russia_2008.pdf

Appendix F

Judicial Branch Oaths of Office:
Supreme Court Justices

According to Title 28, Chapter I, Part 453 of the United States Code, each Supreme Court justice takes the following oath:

"I, [Name], do solemnly swear (or affirm) that I will administer justice without respect to persons, and do equal right to the poor and to the rich, and that I will faithfully and impartially discharge and perform all the duties incumbent upon me as [Title] under the Constitution and laws of the United States. So help me God."

According to 5 U. S. C. § 3331 all federal employees, except the President, must take the following oath:

"I, [Name] do solemnly swear (or affirm) that I will support and defend the Constitution of the United States against all enemies, foreign and domestic; that I will bear true faith and allegiance to the same; that I take this obligation freely, without any mental reservation or purpose of evasion; and that I will well and faithfully discharge the duties of the office on which I am about to enter. So help me God."

Source:

Supreme Court of the United States;
Text of the Oaths of Office for Supreme Court Justices

https://www.supremecourt.gov/about/oath/textoftheoathsofoffice2009.aspx

References

Introduction

1. GPO.gov; List of U.S. Supreme Court Decisions Overruled by Subsequent Decisions.
   https://www.gpo.gov/fdsys/pkg/GPO-CONAN-2002/pdf/GPO-CONAN-2002-12.pdf

2. Federal Judicial Center, Impeachment of Federal Judges.
   https://www.fjc.gov/history/judges/impeachments-federal-judges

Chapter One

Five U.S. Supreme Court Decisions
Regarding Separation of Church & State

1. First Amendment Center, First Amendment Schools;
   Religious Liberty; *Engel v. Vitale, 370 U.S. 421 (1962)*.
   http://www.firstamendmentschools.org/freedoms/case.aspx?id=465

2. First Amendment Center, First Amendment Schools;
   Religious Liberty; *Abington School District v. Schempp, 374 U.S. 203 (1963)*.
   http://www.firstamendmentschools.org/freedoms/case.aspx?id=1238

3. First Amendment Center, First Amendment Schools;
   Religious Liberty; *Stone v. Graham, 449 U.S. 39 (1980)*.

http://www.firstamendmentschools.org/freedoms/case.aspx?
id=1422

4. First Amendment Center, First Amendment Schools;
Religious Liberty; *Lee v. Weisman, 505 U.S. 577 (1992)*.
http://www.firstamendmentschools.org/freedoms/case.aspx?
id=476

5. First Amendment Center, First Amendment Schools;
Religious Liberty: *Santa Fe Independent School District v.
Doe, 530 U.S. 290 (2000)*.
http://www.firstamendmentschools.org/freedoms/case.aspx?
id=489

6. First Amendment Center, First Amendment Schools;
Religious Liberty; *Everson v. Board of Education of Ewing
Township, 330 U.S. 1 (1947)*.
http://www.firstamendmentschools.org/freedoms/case.aspx?
id=467

7. President Ronald Reagan; Radio Address to the Nation on
Prayer, September 18, 1982.
http://www.presidency.ucsb.edu/ws/?pid=43011

Chapter Two

The First 25 Undeniable Facts

1. Virginia Historical Society, Thomas Jefferson and the
Virginia Stature for Religious Freedom.

http://www.vahistorical.org/collections-and-resources/virginia-history-explorer/thomas-jefferson

2. The full text of Thomas Jefferson's 1805 *Second Inaugural Address* can be heard and read on Youtube. https://www.youtube.com/watch?v=KDobcmq3PCc

3. John W. Whitehead, *The Second American Revolution*, Elgin, IL: David C. Cook Publishing Company, 1982, p. 100.

4. Gaillard Hunt, Editor, *Writings of James Madison*, 9 volumes, NY: G. P. Putnam's Sons, 1900-1910, 5: pp. 176 & 132.

5. Letter from James Madison to Robert Walsh, Jr., March 2, 1819. https://founders.archives.gov/documents/Madison/04-01-02-0378

6. John W. Whitehead, *The Second American Revolution*, pp. 99 & 100.

7. John W. Whitehead, *The Second American Revolution*, p. 100.

8. Library of Congress, "Religion and the Founding of the American Republic;" Religion and the Federal Government, Part 2; The State Becomes the Church: Jefferson and Madison. https://www.loc.gov/exhibits/religion/rel06-2.html

9. Christian Heritage Fellowship, "When The United States Capitol Was A Church." https://christianheritagefellowship.com/when-the-united-states-capitol-was-a-church/

10. Wallbuilders, "Church in the U.S. Capitol." https://wallbuilders.com/church-u-s-capitol/

11. Library of Congress, "Religion and the Founding of the American Republic;" Religion and the Federal Government, Part 2; The State Becomes the Church: Jefferson and Madison. https://www.loc.gov/exhibits/religion/rel06-2.html

12. Wallbuilders, "Did George Washington Actually Say 'So Help Me God' During His Inauguration?" https://wallbuilders.com/george-washington-actually-say-help-god-inauguration/

13. Ibid.

14. Ray Soller, American Creation, *"So help me God" – What does it mean?* February 20, 2012; Citing *William and Mary Law Review (1992) Volume 34/Issue 1/13: Religion-Plus-Speech: The Constitutionality of Juror Oaths and Affirmations Under the First Amendment*, by Jonathan Belcher. http://americancreation.blogspot.com/2012/02/so-help-me-god-what-does-it-mean.html

15. Wallbuilders, "The Separation of Church and State." https://wallbuilders.com/separation-church-state/

16. Ibid.

17. Stand To Reason, "Church and State: The Separation Illusion." http://www.str.org/articles/church-and-state-the-separation-illusion#.WXh6uumQyM8

18. Yale Law School; Lillian Goldman Law Library; The Avalon Project: *Documents in Law, History and Diplomacy;* Northwest Ordinance; July 13, 1787; An Ordinance for the government of the Territory of the United States northwest of the Ohio River. http://avalon.law.yale.edu/18th_century/nworder.asp

19. The Free Dictionary; "Northwest Ordinance." http://legal-dictionary.thefreedictionary.com/Northwest+Ordinance+of+1787

20. Message from John Adams to the Officers of the First Brigade of the Third Division of the Militia of Massachusetts – John Adams, October 11, 1798. http://www.beliefnet.com/resourcelib/docs/115/message_from_john_adams_to_the_officers_of_the_first_brigade_1.html

21. William Jay, *The Life of John Jay* (New York: J. & J. Harper, 1833), Vol. II, p. 376, to John Murray, Jr. on October 12, 1816.

22. Patrick Henry, *Patrick Henry: Life, Correspondence and Speeches,* William Wirt Henry, editor (New York: Charles Scribner's Sons, 1891), Vol. II, p. 592, to Archibald Blair on January 8, 1799.

23. Benjamin Rush, *Essays, Literary, Moral & Philosophical* (Philadelphia: Thomas & Samuel F. Bradford, 1798), p. 112, "A Defence of the Use of the Bible as a School Book."

24. Noah Webster, *A Collection of Papers on Political, Literary, and Moral Subjects* (New York: Webster and Clark, 1843), p. 291, from his "Reply to a Letter of David McClure on the Subject of the Proper Course of Study in the Girard College, Philadelphia. New Haven, October 25, 1836."

25. Jedidiah Morse, A Sermon, *Exhibiting the Present Dangers and Consequent Duties of the Citizens of the United States of America*, Delivered at Charlestown, April 25, 1799, The Day of the National Fast (MA: Printed by Samuel Etheridge, 1799), p. 9.

26. Robert Lowry Clinton, *"Marbury v. Madison* and Judicial Review;" University Press of Kansas. https://kansaspress.ku.edu/subjects/history-legal-and-constitutional/978-0-7006-0517-0.html

27. http://freedomkeys.com/vigil.htm

28. 2001 Obama Chicago Public Radio Interview WBEZ.FM. https://www.youtube.com/watch?v=OkpdNtTgQNM

29. The Reverend Patrick J. Conroy, Office of the Chaplain: United States House of Representatives; Religion on the Hill; Congressional Prayer Room. https://chaplain.house.gov/religion/prayer_room.html

30. Positive Quotes.
http://www.quotes-positive.com/quote/saddest-epitaph-carved-memory-vanished-204/

31. Abraham Lincoln Online; Speeches and Writings.
http://www.abrahamlincolnonline.org/lincoln/speeches/gettysburg.htm

32. Library of Congress, Prints and Photographs Online catalog (PPOC). http://www.loc.gov/pictures/item/2008680376/

33. *The American Presidency Project*; Ronald Reagan; Xl President of the United States: 1981 – 1989; Remarks at a Fundraising Dinner Honoring Former Representative John M. Ashbrook in Ashland, Ohio, May 9, 1983.
http://www.presidency.ucsb.edu/ws/index.php?pid=41294

34. Michael W. Chapman, "Bishop Jackson: ACLU-Type Liberals 'Hate God' and 'Hate Christianity,'" CNSNews.com/blog/, March 21, 2017. http://www.cnsnews.com/blog/michael-w-chapman/bp-jackson-aclu-type-liberals-hate-god-any-notion-god-and-they-hate?mkt_tok=eyJpIjoiWkRBME16ZzROelJqTWpNMCIsInQiOiJZdmtCUTJIMkhGcDN5MEUxQTdvZ2lLbWVPV09ReE1NdzIzWVA3dlJMYMYU4zXC8xZU1mUEpiWFwvUU5GSitYckZQK1dweXBYdVFIXC9KWmd5WDRLelQ5cFwvRG12UW9tK2xqWTVjeWVPVVwvMGZncXdZWDZ6cE9nbnpopoS1hYXC9qREJTeHNsNiJ9

35. Mildred Amer, Specialist on the Congress, Congressional Research Service; House and Senate Chaplains; April 25, 2008. https://fas.org/sgp/crs/misc/RS20427.pdf

Chapter Three

The Second 25 Undeniable Facts

1. United States Senate; Art and History; Chaplain of the Senate. https://www.senate.gov/artandhistory/history/common/generic/People_Chaplain.htm

2. Mildred Amer, Specialist on the Congress, Congressional Research Service; House and Senate Chaplains; April 25, 2008. https://fas.org/sgp/crs/misc/RS20427.pdf

3. Ibid.

4. The Reverend Patrick J. Conroy, Office of the Chaplain: United States House of Representatives; The Chaplaincy. https://chaplain.house.gov/chaplaincy/index.html

5. Mildred Amer, Specialist on the Congress, Congressional Research Service; House and Senate Chaplains; April 25, 2008. https://fas.org/sgp/crs/misc/RS20427.pdf

6. Floor Action 5 – 145; Prayer Practices. http://www.ncsl.org/documents/legismgt/ILP/02Tab5Pt7.pdf

7. Floor Action 5 – 145; Prayer Practices. http://www.ncsl.org/documents/legismgt/ILP/02Tab5Pt7.pdf

8. Jim Allison, Revisiting *Marsh v. Chambers.*
    http://candst.tripod.com/marshchm.htm

9. Georgetown University; Berkley Center for Religion, Peace
    & World Affairs; Resources on Faith, Ethics & Public Life;
    Marsh v. Chambers.
    https://berkleycenter.georgetown.edu/cases/marsh-v-
    chambers--2

10. The Judicial View; Court Decision Research & Alerts; Federal
    Cases; A Publication of the Judicial View, LLC; *Marsh v.
    Chambers 463 U.S. 783.* https://judicialview.com/Court-
    Cases/Government_Politics/Marsh-v.-
    Chambers/28/277670

11. William Z. Foster, *Toward Soviet America*, Balboa Island, CA:
    Elgin Publications, 1961, p. 317. (Originally published in
    1932).

12. William Z. Foster, *Toward Soviet America*, p. 316.

13. "The Right Stuff," *The New American*, August 08, 1994.

14. William Z. Foster, National Chairman of the Communist
    Party, USA, quoting Vladimir Lenin. Source: William Z.
    Foster, *Toward Soviet America*, Balboa Islands, CA: Elgin
    Publications, 1961, p. 134. (Originally published in 1932).

15. W. Cleon Skousen, *The Naked Communist,* Eleventh
    Edition, Salt Lake City, UT: The Reviewer, 1962, p. 261.

16. Newsmax.com, Communist Goals; May 08, 2003.
http://www.newsmax.com/Pre-2008/Communist-
Goals/2003/05/08/id/675822/

17. Alan Sears, "ACLU's Shocking Legacy," WorldNetDaily.com,
August 25, 2005.
http://www.wnd.com/2005/08/31979/

18. Matt Barber, "ACLU: Communism is the Goal," March 25,
2011, Townhall.com;
https://townhall.com/columnists/mattbarber/2011/03/25/a
clu-communism-is-the-goal-n1167720

19. DiscoverTheNetworks.org; A Guide to the Political Left;
Roger Baldwin.
http://www.discoverthenetworks.org/individualProfile.asp?i
ndid=1579

20. Devvy Kidd, "ACLU fulfilling Communist agenda,"
WorldNetDaily.com, December 03, 2004.

21. Linda P. Campbell, *Chicago Tribune;* "Ginsburg Confirmed
For Court On 96-3 Vote," August 04, 1993.
http://articles.chicagotribune.com/1993-08-
04/news/9308040122_1_ruth-bader-ginsburg-supreme-
court-abortion-protesters

22. Cornell University Law School; Legal Information Institute;
Supreme Court; *Santa Fe Independent School District v.
Doe 530 U.S. 290 (2000) 168F.3d 806,* affirmed.
https://www.law.cornell.edu/supct/html/99-62.ZD.html

23. Reagan Library; Remarks at an Ecumenical Prayer Breakfast in Dallas, Texas, August 23, 1984. https://reaganlibrary.archives.gov/archives/speeches/1984/82384a.htm

24. Anatoly V. Lunarcharsky, Russian Commissar of Education. Source: Anatoly V. Lunarcharsky, Russian Commissar of Education, *U.S. Congressional Record*, Volume 77, pp. 1539-1540, cited in *The Naked Communist*, Eleventh Edition, Salt Lake City, UT: The Reviewer, 1962, p. 308.

25. Heritage.us; Pictures of 10 Commandments; Pictures of the Ten Commandments and Moses at the United States Supreme Court Building. http://www.heritage-signs.us/ten/more_info.phtml

26. David G. Savage, *Los Angeles Times*, "Marshall Eulogized as 'Rock of Justice': Tribute: In services at Washington National Cathedral, former law clerks and friends recalled the jurist as a visionary who never gave up hope;" January 29, 1993. http://articles.latimes.com/1993-01-29/news/mn-2028_1_washington-national-cathedral

27. Jay Sekulow, ACLJ; Supreme Court; "God Save The United States and This Honorable Court." https://aclj.org/supreme-court-justices/god-save-the-united-states-and-this-honorable-court

28. U.S. Constitution; God in the State Constitutions. https://www.usconstitution.net/states_god.html

29. ProCon.org; References to "God" in State Constitutions. http://undergod.procon.org/view.resource.php?resourceID=000081

30. TimeAndDate.com; "National Day of Prayer in the United States."
    https://www.timeanddate.com/holidays/us/national-day-prayer

31. NationalDayOfPrayer.org; National Day Of Prayer.
    http://www.nationaldayofprayer.org/about

32. The Fellowship Foundation: Also Known as the International Foundation; Assisting with the National Prayer Breakfast and Other Gatherings.
    http://thefellowshipfoundation.org/activities.html

33. Smithsonian.com; "The History of the National Prayer Breakfast."
    http://www.smithsonianmag.com/history/national-prayer-breakfast-what-does-its-history-reveal-180962017/

34. Cathedral.org; Washington National Cathedral; Timeline; The dream of a national cathedral dates back to the earliest days of the United States, when President George Washington and architect Pierre L'Enfant imagined a "great church for national purposes."
    https://cathedral.org/history/timeline/

35. History.com; Washington, D.C.; Article; Interesting Facts.
    http://www.history.com/topics/us-states/washington-dc

36. NPS.gov; National Park Service, U.S. Department of the Interior, Washington, D.C.: National Cathedral.
    https://www.nps.gov/nr/travel/wash/dc5.htm

37. Amanda Ripley, Content.Time.com; Washington: 10 Things to Do; 6. Washington National Cathedral. http://content.time.com/time/travel/cityguide/article/0,314 89,1852610_1852670_1852638,00.html

38. Cathedral.org; Washington National Cathedral; https://cathedral.org/history/timeline/

39. Wallbuilders.com; "The Separation of Church and State." https://wallbuilders.com/separation-church-state/

40. Heritage.org; The Heritage Foundation; Report: Political Process; "The Mythical 'Wall of Separation:' How A Misused Metaphor Changes Church-State Law, Policy, and Discourse." June 23, 2006. http://www.heritage.org/political-process/report/the-mythical-wall-separation-how-misused-metaphor-changed-church-state-law

41. First Amendment Center, First Amendment Schools; Religious Liberty; *Engel v. Vitale, 370 U.S. 421 (1962)*. http://www.firstamendmentschools.org/freedoms/case.aspx ?id=465

42. First Amendment Center, First Amendment Schools; Religious Liberty; *Stone v. Graham, 449 U.S. 39 (1980)*. http://www.firstamendmentschools.org/freedoms/case.aspx ?id=1422

43. First Amendment Center, First Amendment Schools;
Religious Liberty; *Lee v. Weisman, 505 U.S. 577 (1992)*.
http://www.firstamendmentschools.org/freedoms/case.aspx
?id=476

44. First Amendment Center, First Amendment Schools;
Religious Liberty; *Santa Fe Independent School District v.
Doe, 530 U.S. 290 (2000)*.
http://www.firstamendmentschools.org/freedoms/case.aspx
?id=489

Chapter Four

The Johnson Amendment & The IRS

1. Michelle Terry, ACLJ.org; "How the Johnson Amendment
    Threatens Churches' Freedoms." https://aclj.org/free-
    speech/how-the-johnson-amendment-threatens-churches-
    freedoms

2. Lee Duigon, "Do Churches Need 501 (C)(3) Status?"
    Resources, Chalcedon, February 10, 2006.
    https://chalcedon.edu/resources/articles/do-churches-
    need-501c3-status

3. Tom McGregor, "Catholicism in China Today," *Crisis
    Magazine;* August 15, 2013.
    http://www.crisismagazine.com/2013/catholicism-in-china-
    today

4. Lee Duigon, "Do Churches Need 501 (C)(3) Status?" Resources, Chalcedon, February 10, 2006. https://chalcedon.edu/resources/articles/do-churches-need-501c3-status

5. Erik W. Stanley, "Are Churches Subject to Section 501(C)(3) of the Tax Code?" Alliance Defending Freedom; February 27, 2012. https://www.adflegal.org/detailspages/blog-details/allianceedge/2012/02/27/are-churches-subject-to-section-501(c)(3)-of-the-tax-code

6. Judge Andrew P. Napolitano, *The Constitution In Exile: How the Federal Government Has Seized Power by Rewriting the Supreme Law of The Land,* Nashville, TN: Thomas Nelson, 2006, p. 233.

7. Judson Berger, "Trump vows to protect religious liberty – and knocks Arnold – at National Prayer Breakfast," FoxNews.com, Fox News Politics; February 02, 2017. http://www.foxnews.com/politics/2017/02/02/trump-vows-to-protect-religious-liberty-and-knocks-arnold-at-national-prayer-breakfast.html

8. Jennifer Wishon, "HISTORIC: Trump Restores Religious Rights and Protects Pastors on Day of Prayer;" CBN News, Politics, May 04, 2017. http://www1.cbn.com/cbnnews/politics/2017/may/trump-ready-to-sign-religious-freedom-order-on-national-day-of-prayer

9. Erik W. Stanley, *Regent University Law Review*, Volume 24, 2011-2012, Number 2; LBJ, "The IRS, And Churches: The Unconstitutionality of the Johnson Amendment in Light of Recent Supreme Court Precedent." http://www.blackrobereg.org/uploads/2/8/9/8/2898266/01 stanleyvol.24.2.pdf

10. The Horn News, "Trump's Master Plan Revealed," February 27, 2017. https://thehornnews.com/trumps-master-plan-revealed/

11. Cliff Kincaid, "Dismantling the Marxist Madrassas," Accuracy In Media, AIM.org, May 15, 2017. http://www.aim.org/aim-column/dismantling-the-marxist-madrassas/

Chapter Five

The Sinister Goal Behind
"Separation of Church and State"

1. Vladimir Lenin, in *Lenin: Selected Works*, cited at: http://www.ewtn.com/library/PROLENC/ENCYC094.HTM

2. Proverbia.net, Edmund Burke. http://en.proverbia.net/citasautor.asp?autor=11154&page=6

3. Acton Institute; Religion & Liberty: Volume 7, Number 1; "Edmund Burke," July 20, 2010. https://acton.org/pub/religion-liberty/volume-7-number-1/edmund-burke

4. Testimony before the U.S. Department of Education, cited in *Child Abuse in the Classroom*, Phyllis Schlafly, Editor, Westchester, IL: Crossway Books, 1988, p. 57.

5. Testimony before the U.S. Department of Education, cited in *Child Abuse in the Classroom*, p. 244.

6. *Child Abuse in the Classroom*, p. 99.

7. Linus Wright, "Sex Education: How to Respond," *The World & I*, September 1989, p. 515.

8. Thomas Sowell, *Inside American Education: The Decline, The Deception, The Dogmas*, New York: The Free Press, 1993.

9. Thomas Sowell, *Inside American Education: The Decline, The Deception, The Dogmas*, p. 65.

10. *Child Abuse in the Classroom*, p. 53.

11. William Kilpatrick, *Why Johnny Can't Tell Right From Wrong: Moral Illiteracy and the Case for Character Education*, NY: Simon & Schuster, 1992.

12. William J. Bennett, excerpts from *What Really Ails America*, condensed from a December 7, 1993 speech he delivered at the Heritage Foundation, Washington, D.C., and reprinted in *Reader's Digest*, April, 1994.

13. William F. Jasper, "The State of Our Decline: A Postmortem on Public Education," *The New American*, August 08, 1994.

14. J. Edgar Hoover, *J. Edgar Hoover On Communism*, NY: Random House, 1970, p. 152.

15. Pastor Ernie Sanders, *WRWL (What's Right, What's Left) Radio Ministries;* Radio Talk Show Host on WHWW-1220am, WHKZ-1440am, WRSB-1310am, WASB-1570am. Doers of the Word Baptist Church, 14781 Sperry Road, Newbury, Ohio 44065.

16. R. J. Rummel, *Death By Government*, New Brunswick, N.J.: Transaction Publisher, 1994. https://www.hawaii.edu/powerkills/NOTE1.HTM

17. William Z. Foster, "Syndicalism," p. 9. In W. Cleon Skousen, *The Naked Communist*, Eleventh Edition, Salt Lake City, UT: The Reviewer, 1962, p. 305.

18. William Z. Foster, *Toward Soviet America*, Balboa Island, CA: Elgin Publications, 1961, p. 316. (Originally published in 1932).

19. William Z. Foster, *Toward Soviet America*, p. 316.

20. W. Cleon Skousen, *The Naked Communist*, Eleventh Edition, Salt Lake City, UT: The Reviewer, 1962, p. 261.

Chapter Six

Numerous Misjudgments by the U.S. Supreme Court have Fostered Widespread Hostility Towards Religious Liberty in The United States of America

1. Family Research Council; "Hostility to Religion: The Growing Threat to Religious Liberty in the United States," June 2017 Edition.
   http://downloads.frc.org/EF/EF17F51.pdf

2. Todd Starnes; "Teens Threatened with Arrest for Praying – In America!" Townhall.com, June 30, 2017.
   https://townhall.com/columnists/toddstarnes/2017/06/30/teens-threatened-with-arrest-for-praying--in-america-n2348756?utm_source=thdaily&utm_medium=email&utm_campaign=nl&newsletterad=

3. Family Research Council, "A Clear and Present Danger: The Threat to Religious Liberty in the Military – Volume II."
   http://www.frc.org/clearpresentdanger2

4. Cortney O'Brien, "Football Coach Defies School District Warning, Prays for Team at Homecoming Game," Townhall.com, October 17, 2015.
   https://townhall.com/tipsheet/cortneyobrien/2015/10/17/football-coach-defies-school-district-warning-prays-for-team-at-homecoming-game-n2066512

5. Cortney O'Brien, "Football Coach Fired For Praying With Team Turns Tables on School District," August 9, 2016. https://townhall.com/tipsheet/cortneyobrien/2016/08/09/f ootball-coach-fired-for-praying-with-team-turns-tables-on-school-district-n2203386

6. United States District Court, Western District of Washington at Tocoma. *Joseph A. Kennedy, Plaintiff, v. Bremerton School District, Defendant.* FirstLiberty.org. http://firstliberty.org/wp-content/uploads/2016/08/Filed-Complaint.pdf

7. Todd Starnes, "Franklin Graham: 'We Have Judges Out There Who Hate God...'" Townhall.com, August 25, 2017. https://townhall.com/columnists/toddstarnes/2017/08/25/ franklin-graham-we-have-judges-out-there-who-hate-god-n2372994

8. Todd Starnes, "School: Praying for a Colleague is Unacceptable," Townhall.com, May16, 2017. https://townhall.com/columnists/toddstarnes/2017/05/16/ school-praying-for-a-colleague-is-unacceptable-n2327587

9. Memorandum, Cony High School, Augusta, Maine, FirstLiberty.org, September 19, 2016. https://firstliberty.org/wp-content/uploads/2017/05/Coaching-Memorandum-Toni-Richardson-05.16.17.pdf

10. Todd Starnes, "Sheriff Ordered to Remove 'Blessed are the Peacemakers' Decals," Fox News, *Fox News Opinion*, May 19, 2017.

http://www.foxnews.com/opinion/2017/05/19/sheriff-
ordered-to-remove-blessed-are-peacemakers-decals.html

11. Jenn Jacques, "Sheriff Ordered to Remove 'Blessed are the
    Peacemakers' Decals from vehicles," Bearing Arms.com,
    May 24, 2017. https://bearingarms.com/jenn-
    j/2017/05/24/sheriff-ordered-to-remove-blessed-are-the-
    peacekeepers-decals-from-
    vehicles/?utm_source=thdailypm&utm_medium=email&ut
    m_campaign=nl_pm&newsletterad=

12. Mike Gangloff, "Bible Verse Decals to Come Off Patrol Cars
    Immediately, Montgomery County Sheriff says," *The
    Roanoke Times,* May 17, 2017.
    http://www.roanoke.com/news/local/montgomery_county
    /bible-verse-decals-to-come-off-patrol-cars-soon-
    montgomery/article_2c4f208b-4a5e-55a0-b98e-
    8a5eaaa6d5c8.html

13. John Chase, "Graduates Skirt Prayer Ban," *Chicago Tribune,*
    May 21, 2001. http://articles.chicagotribune.com/2001-
    05-21/news/0105210103_1_silent-prayer-invocation-and-
    benediction-graduating

Chapter Seven

It's Time to Impeach Corrupt Judges,
including those sitting on
the U.S. Supreme Court

1. Quotes by...? Margaret Thatcher Quotes, Quotesby.net.
   http://www.quotesby.net/Margaret-Thatcher

2. Cliff Kincaid, "It's Time to Impeach the Judges," Accuracy In
   Media, AIM.org, February 13, 2017.
   http://www.aim.org/aim-column/its-time-to-impeach-
   the-judges/

3. Federal Judicial Center; Judges; History of the Federal
   Judiciary, Impeachments of Federal Judges.
   https://www.fjc.gov/history/judges/impeachments-federal-
   judges

4. GPO.gov; List of U.S. Supreme Court Decisions Overruled
   by Subsequent Decisions.
   https://www.gpo.gov/fdsys/pkg/GPO-CONAN-
   2002/pdf/GPO-CONAN-2002-12.pdf

5. Library of Congress, Prints and Photographs Online
   Catalog (PPOC).
   http://www.loc.gov/pictures/item/2008680376/

6. William Z. Foster, *Toward Soviet America,* Balboa Island,
   CA: Elgin Publications, 1961. (Originally published in 1932);
   pp. 135-136.

7. Nicholas Ballasy, "Ron Paul: GOP Leaders Need to Read
   Constitution," CNSNews.com, March 11, 2009.

Chapter Eight

A Few Important, Final Thoughts

1. Jonathan Turley, Opinion: "Don Jr.'s Russia Meeting Wasn't Collusion – Just Amateur Hour," TheHill.com, July 17, 2017. http://thehill.com/blogs/pundits-blog/the-administration/341461-opinion-don-jrs-russia-meeting-wasnt-collusion-just

2. Alan Dershowitz One-On-One Explosive Interview with Judge Jeanine Pirro; Youtube.com, August 15, 2017. https://www.youtube.com/watch?v=YjqxLE6thZI

3. David Kopel, "Sotomayor targets guns now: justice's dissent contradicts confirmation testimony," *The Washington Times*, Tuesday, June 29, 2010. http://www.washingtontimes.com/news/2010/jun/29/sotomayor-targets-guns-now/

4. Buckeye Firearms Association; "Gun Quotes of the Founding Fathers," BuckeyeFirearms.org. https://www.buckeyefirearms.org/gun-quotations-founding-fathers

5. Guardian.co.uk. Guardian News and Media Limited 2011. https://www.theguardian.com/notesandqueries/query/0,5753,-21510,00.html

About the Author

Michael T. Petro, Jr. is a veteran of the U.S. Navy. Initially he worked in naval security, and later served in the gunnery division aboard the USS Kennebec during the Vietnam War. After returning to his native state of Ohio, he earned a Bachelor of Arts degree (Magna Cum Laude) from Cleveland State University.

When relocating to California he earned a Master of Science degree in Psychology and a Master of Arts degree in Education from California State University at Los Angeles. Michael initially worked as an aide and counselor in psychiatric hospitals in the greater Los Angeles area. Later he worked extensively as a researcher, training coordinator, and manager at an alcohol and drug recovery program located on Skid Row in Los Angeles.

Before leaving California, Michael received a National Leadership Award from the National Headquarters of the Volunteers of America. The award was presented for his success in restoring operational integrity to a dysfunctional alcohol and drug recovery program and for his efforts to create drug-free zones within the Skid Row community.

Today, Michael works as a writer, editor, and publisher in Cleveland, Ohio, helping aspiring writers become published authors. For more information visit PetroPublications.com.